Hebrew Lessons

for

Beginners

from the

New Testament

Rosamund Weissman

(with contributions from

Robert Weissman)

Hebrew Lessons

for Beginners

from the

New Testament

Published by Fresh Olive Press
fresholivepress.com

ISBN 978-1-8382347-0-6
First printing 2022
Printed in the United Kingdom

Book cover design by Jonathan Weissman
Cover image sourced from pexels.com

Contents

Dedication

This book is dedicated to the intercessors who read my companion work "Exploring the End Times and Praying for Israel." I am aware that the subject matter of that book will have placed a heavy burden upon them. "Hebrew Lessons for Beginners from the New Testament" is presented to put smiles on their faces and, in that sense, lighten their load!

Note about set-up

The book is designed to accommodate both those who want to read the Hebrew text and those content to read a transliteration.[1]Accordingly, those readers who wish to practise their reading skills can make use of a strip of paper to obscure the transliteration. There are two ways of approaching the material in these lessons. You can either work through the book consecutively, only moving on when you have mastered the alphabet, or you can start at Lesson 3 and use the first two lessons as reference material.

---

[1] Use of English characters to approximate pronunciation of a word from another language.

Preface

This is written for Christians who want to learn Hebrew and who desire to deepen their understanding of the Hebraic background of the New Testament. This teaching is humbly offered to contribute towards "the equipping of the saints for the work of ministry, for the edifying of the body of Christ."[2]

The New Testament contains a treasury of Hebrew thoughts and truths, thinly concealed beneath the so-familiar text. These gems are presented and examined through the medium of 12 beginners' Hebrew lessons. Each lesson can be approached in one of two ways. They are suitable for those who wish to learn or revise beginner's Hebrew. Alternatively, the English text can be read and appreciated in its own right (making use of the transliterations), without studying the Hebrew reading component. Whether you are reading this book to build up your knowledge of Biblical or modern Hebrew, or to inspire you in poetry, song, or craft activities, may you be blessed!

I am deeply indebted to my husband Robert for his contributions to the later chapters. These have been written by him from the perspective of almost fifty years' experience as an evangelist to Jewish people, and as a Christian preacher and teacher, presenting the Hebrew background to the Old and New Testaments. Many thanks also to family and friends for their patient help in editing and proof reading the text, and with the book cover design.

---

[2] Ephesians 4:12

Note for Bible College students and disclaimer

The purpose of this book is to inspire Christians to take the first steps in understanding Hebrew. It is also presented to enrich the understanding of Christian readers of the New Testament. It is neither designed, nor intended, for use by serious Bible College students sitting examinations and evaluations. If you are in this category of reader, please enjoy what I have written, but do not treat this devotional book as a rigorous scholarly resource. It is written from a casual background of a favourite hobby – learning Hebrew, and not from the standpoint of classical, academic language study. In researching and writing this book, I have typically gone with the consensus of various internet articles readily available online. For this reason, there is scant use of bibliographical sources. If this book motivates you to further your formal academic studies, then it has done its job!

My Hebrew language story

I must confess to being a person who disliked learning languages at school. I approached French lessons as one would learn Latin (not that I was good enough at French to be picked to study Latin). To me, French was a list of grammatical rules which I learned to the best of my ability, and it was outside my teenage awareness that anyone actually spoke this language in their regular lives. I intently disliked learning German and barely scraped an O Level, which frankly I did not deserve.

When I was 18, I spent eight months in Israel and attended a Kibbutz Hebrew learning course, called an *Ulpan*. I adapted far better to this, especially as there were at least two people on our course who could not speak English – one from Morocco and one from Russia – and Hebrew was spoken all around us. So Hebrew was obviously the best means of communication in such a situation. I made quick progress and was moved from the beginners to the more advanced group.

I returned to the UK and I have written about my testimony of coming to faith from a Jewish background in my book, "Exploring the End Times and Interceding for Israel." Most of this testimony is available on my Fresh Olive Press website.[3] Some months after I received the Lord Jesus as my personal Saviour, He led me back to visit Israel over my summer vacation from university. One day on that trip, I was walking around Caesarea, where some relatives lived. Suddenly (and I can clearly recall the place where this happened), I was able to speak out with a non-British and attractive accent, and to string together fluently the modest amount of Hebrew which I knew. It was hardly the gift of tongues described in

---

[3] https://www.fresholivepress.com/testimony-and-introduction

the book of Acts because, if I did not know a word or whether the word was masculine or feminine, I was stuck. Nevertheless, in an instant, I could use what Hebrew I had learned to converse, provided the other participant did not shower me in return with words and phrases which I had not heard before! I was very happy, like a tone-deaf person who could suddenly sing in tune. So, enthusiastically over the decades which followed, I built up my Hebrew understanding through watching Israeli films with English subtitles and attending the occasional online Ulpan course. I enjoy praying in Hebrew and listening to Hebrew worship songs. About 10 years ago, I started teaching beginners' Hebrew to adults at the Tree of Life Messianic Fellowship in Ilford in east London, and this continued for a few years. I am still only at an intermediate level myself and I understand that in Israel, it is not unusual for someone who had to learn Hebrew for themselves to teach complete beginners, because they understand how hard the language is to get to grips with! Over the years, I have pondered upon the reason why the Lord gave me this experience back in 1977. Initially, I assumed that it was part of His leading to prepare me to go and live in Israel. That never happened, and yet Hebrew became one of my favourite pastimes. As I consider this book, I can testify that these writings are the fruit of what occurred that day. May its pages bring blessings to the reader!

Introduction

Eliezer Ben Yehuda was a major force in reviving the use of Hebrew from a study language to a spoken one. He accomplished this over a period of about forty years, following his arrival in the Land in 1881. His primary source for accurate vocabulary was the Hebrew Scriptures, which we know as the Old Testament. If the word he was searching for was not there, then he would look to sister languages for inspiration or indeed make up the words, like the Hebrew for "pencil" or "bicycle."[4] It is for this reason that, as we go through this book, we can learn to read certain Hebrew nouns, confident that they are just as useful in understanding Biblical Hebrew as in modern conversation with Israelis. This also gives options to the reader. The lessons may provide you with interesting Hebrew words and insights to make use of in ministry, preaching, teaching, artwork, craft, prayer, poetry, or songs. They may spark an interest in serious study of Old Testament Hebrew. Perhaps some readers will decide to pursue studies in modern Hebrew. To avoid confusion, this book will not deal with the verb structure and other grammatical details which differ between Biblical and modern spoken Hebrew. Before we start, let me draw attention to "the elephant in the room!" It is generally accepted that the New Testament was written originally in Koine Greek, which is an older form of the Greek language spoken at that time.[5] So it is not obvious to use the New Testament as a resource for Hebrew lessons for beginners. We are taking this approach to give a well-defined scope and context for our studies. We need to keep in mind during

---

[4] I strongly recommend reading the book, "Tongue of the Prophets the life story of Eliezer Ben Yehuda" by Robert St. John

[5] It is beyond the scope of this book to examine alternative positions concerning the existence of earlier Hebrew manuscripts

these lessons that Aramaic was the local language spoken in the Land of Israel during New Testament times. It was the mother tongue of Jesus. Since the New Testament manuscripts are in Greek, it is not always easy to distinguish where the writers are referring to Hebrew or Aramaic words and phrases.

Lesson 1: Hebrew letters and vowels

Hebrew is read from right to left, and there is no such thing as upper or lower case; it is all capitals. A Bible or book written in Hebrew starts at what we would consider the back of the book and ends at what we would regard as the beginning. The Old Testament books were written almost entirely in Hebrew without vowels.[6] Jewish scribes working in the 6th to 10th centuries AD helpfully added vowels to the Bible, thus producing the Masoretic text. These are written as differing marks mainly under the letters.

When we look at Hebrew usage today, books and literature designed for new immigrants to Israel, and for young children learning to read, will typically have the consonants accompanied by the vowel points. Vowels are subsequently gradually withdrawn except for new words where they are inserted at first for pronunciation purposes. Books written for teenagers and older people will merely have the 22 consonants from the Hebrew alphabet, leaving the reader to work out the vowels from the context. This is not difficult for someone experienced in the language. Consider the English language, and take three consonants, "b" "n" and "d." If you read a sentence which left the vowel out of a relevant word, so that it said "bnd," you could easily work out from the context whether the word should read band, bend, bind or bond. So, if you read, "Since injuring my back, it is painful to "bnd" down," you would instantly know what the word is with the missing vowel.

If we try and imagine what it is like for native speakers reading Hebrew without vowels, then the title of this book "Hebrew Lessons for Beginners from the New Testament"

---

[6] There are also a few passages written in Aramaic, mainly in the books of Ezra and Daniel.

would read something like this (reading from the right to the left):

TNMTST WN HT MRF SRNNGB RF SNSSL WRBH

If we now go on to a well-known expression, "an apple a day keeps the doctor away," some of the words here start with a vowel. Vowels are generally under a letter in Hebrew, and if the vowel is the first sound in a word, then it will have to be one of the two silent letters, which we will go on to learn about. So, in the following illustration, I have represented the silent letters with pairs of square brackets. The reader will need to imagine the missing "a" under each of them.

YW[ ] RTCD HT SPK YD [ ] LPP[ ] N[ ]

If you are new to Hebrew, you can start by writing your name from right to left just using the Hebrew consonants in this lesson's Hebrew Alphabet chart. If your name includes one of the sounds or letters excluded from the Hebrew alphabet, like "ch," "th," "j" or "w," you can try spelling out something else. Some Hebrew letters have a special form when they appear at the end of a word, and the final letters are indicated in the chart. So, if like me, your surname ends with "man," then the "n" will be in the form of the final *nun*, the *nun sofit*. You will be relieved to know that throughout this book designed for complete beginners, we shall be making full use of the vowels!

Some of the 22 letters of the Hebrew alphabet can be read in one of two ways, depending on the use of a dot inside the letter, called a *dagesh*. The alternative reading of these letters (depending on the dots) is shaded in the chart.[7] The Hebrew grammar rules about the *dagesh* are extremely complex. The

---

[7] There are more than 22 rows in the chart due to the alternative readings and also the final letters.

sort of *dagesh* which changes the basic sound of the letter, as described, is a *weak dagesh*. There is another sort of *dagesh*, which produces a doubling of the letter in which it is contained, which is called a *strong dagesh*.[8]

As you study the chart, I would add that there is no "th" nor "ch" sound like we have in English. So, when we read a name in English in the Bible, like "Goliath" or "Bethel," in Hebrew, the "th" would simply be pronounced as "t." Similarly, if we read "cherub," or King Chedorlaomer,[9] we need to bear in mind that the "ch" sound is representing the letter *kaf*.

---

[8] Some readers may wonder if a dot within a letter (say *beit* or *peh*) can both identify the sound of the letter (like a *weak dagesh*) and also double the sound (like a *strong dagesh*). The answer is "yes," it is possible for one *dagesh* to perform both functions, like in the Hebrew word *Shabbat*. Those readers who enjoy fine grammatical details may like to further investigate the *dagesh lene* (weak) and the *dagesh forte* (strong). The *dalet, gimel* and *tav* must have a *dagesh* if they appear at the start of a word. There the *dagesh* makes no difference to the pronunciation.

[9] Genesis 14:4

Hebrew Alphabet Chart

Letter	Name	Transliteration	Sound
א	אָלֶף	alef	silent
בּ	בֵּית	beit	b
ב	בֵית	veit	v
ג	גִּימֶל	gimel	g
ד	דָּלֶת	dalet	d
ה	הֵי	hey	h
ו	וָו	vav	v or o
ז	זַיִן	zayin	z
ח	חֵית	khet	"kh" as in "ch" of loch
ט	טֵית	tet	t
י	יוֹד	yod	y
כ	כָּף	kaf	k

כ	כָף	khaf	"kh" as in "ch" of loch
ך	כָּף סוֹפִית	kaf-sofit	final kaf
ל	לָמֶד	lamed	l
מ	מֶם	mem	m
ם	מֶם סוֹפִית	mem-sofit	final mem
נ	נוּן	nun	n
ן	נוּן סוֹפִית	nun-sofit	final nun
ס	סָמֶךְ	samech	s
ע	עַיִן	ayin	silent
פ	פֵּא	pay	p
פ	פֵא	fay	f
ף	פֵא סוֹפִית	pay-sofit (usually "f" sound)	final pay
צ	צָדִי	tsadee	"ts" as in <u>ts</u>ar

ץ	צָדִי סוֹפִית	tsadee-sofit	final tsadee
ק	קוֹף	kof	k
ר	רֵישׁ	raysh	r
שׁ	שִׁין	shin	sh
שׂ	שִׂין	sin	s
ת	תָּו	tav	t

Hebrew Vowel Chart

Vowel	Name	Transliteration	Sound
אְ	שְׁוָא	shv'h	silent or short "e"
אַ	פַּתָּח	patakh	"ah" as in f<u>a</u>ther
אָ	קָמֵץ	kamats	"ah" as in f<u>a</u>ther*
אֲ	חֲטַף פַּתָּח	khataf patakh	shorter "a" as in m<u>a</u>t
אֶ	סֶגוֹל	segol	"eh" as in m<u>e</u>t
אֵ	צֵירֵי	tsere	"eh" as in m<u>e</u>t
אִ	חִירִיק	kheereek	"i" as in l<u>i</u>t or "ee" as in s<u>ee</u>ms
אֹ	חוֹלָם	kholam	"o" as in <u>o</u>n
אוֹ	חוֹלָם וָו	kholam vav	"o" as in <u>o</u>n
אוּ	שׁוּרוּק	shoor-ook	"oo" as in m<u>oo</u>d
אֻ	קֻבּוּץ	kooboots	"oo" as in m<u>oo</u>d

אִי	חִירִיק יוֹד	kheereek yod	"ee" as in b<u>ee</u>
אֵי	צֵירֵי יוֹד	tsere yod	"ay" as in m<u>ay</u>
אַי	פַּתָח יוֹד	patakh yod	"ie" as in t<u>ie</u>

* Occasionally, it has an "o" sound; then the vowel is called a *kamats katan* (small *kamats*). Examples that may crop up in looking at the Scriptures are the words for "all" and "wisdom," pronounced *kol* and *khokhmah*. See reading chart in the following chapter.

Lesson 2: How to read Hebrew

This lesson is very detailed. You have a choice of how to use this material, depending on learning style and personality. If you are a person who enjoys carefully building foundations to studies, then start with this lesson. However, if you are eager to read about the Hebrew content of the New Testament, then go ahead to Lesson 3 and beyond, and use the information here as reference material to assist you and perhaps to study when you have read the whole book.

Below is a reading lesson study chart relating to the different letters in Hebrew alphabetical order, and you can cover the transliteration column if that suits you.

Reading notes	Meaning	Sound	Hebrew
1st letter is silent, start with vowel underneath. No dot in 2nd letter so "v"	father	av	אָב
2nd letter has *dagesh* or dot, so "b", followed by vowel underneath	daddy	ab-ba	אַבָּא
The two vertical dots *shv'h* show a break in sounds, notice the *mem sofit*	Exalted father	Av-ram	אַבְרָם
Notice insertion of the *hey*	Father of a multitude	Av-ra-ham	אַבְרָהָם
First letter has *dagesh* dot so b	house	ba-yit	בַּיִת

The vowel under the *beit* combines with *yod* to make "ey" sound.	House of Bread (Bethlehem)	Beyt-Lekhem	בֵּית לֶחֶם
The dot on the *shin* is on the right side, so "sh"	House of the Sun	Beyt-Shemesh	בֵּית שֶׁמֶשׁ
The *a* sound is under a silent letter. Notice use of the *nun sofit*	Place of Quiet	Beyt-Sh'ean	בֵּית שְׁאָן
Ignore *dagesh* in 1st letter	roof	gag	גָּג
The vowel here is a dot above the letter *vav*	Ezekiel 38:2	Gog	גּוֹג
The *shv'h* shows a break in sounds	wheel	gal-gal	גַּלְגַּל
Notice the *nun sofit*	garden	gan	גַּן
Ignore *dagesh* in 1st letter	fish	dag	דָּג
Ignore *dagesh* in 1st letter	door	delet	דֶּלֶת
The absence of the *dagesh* makes the middle letter *v*	word	davar	דָּבָר
Notice the *mem sofit*	blood	dam	דָּם
A simple word to read	mountain	har	הַר
The *dagesh* doubles the letter	behold	hinneh	הִנֵּה
The *aleph* at the end is totally silent	he	hoo	הוּא

"who" means "he" and "he" means "she"	she	hee	הִיא
No dots on or in the *vavs* so both pronounced "v"	hook, peg	vav	וָו
1st syllable closes with the *shv'h*	beautiful one	Vash-ti	וַשְׁתִּי
Here the *vav* has a dot above it, so it is an "o" sound	light	or	אוֹר
[a simple word to read]	this	zeh	זֶה
Slight pause after 1st vowel *shv'h*	time	z'man	זְמַן
[Easy word to read]	gold	za-hav	זָהָב
These two different vowels have the same "e" sound	memorial	zekher	זֵכֶר
The *khet* is a guttural sound like the "ch" in "loch"	friend	khaver	חָבֵר
[Again a simple word]	festival	khag	חַג
Notice the final letter *pey sofit* pronounced "f"	shore	khof	חוֹף
The *khet* and the *khaf* have the same sound.	wise	kha-kham	חָכָם

kamats katan produces an "o" sound not "a"	wisdom	khokh-mah	חָכְמָה
Notice absence of *dagesh*, so "v" sound at end	good	tov	טוֹב
Also a Hebrew name	dew	tal	טַל
Note how the word contains both of the "t" letters	10th month[10]	tevet	טֵבֵת
Notice *mem sofit*	taste	ta-am	טַעַם
[this is the primary meaning of word]	hand	yad	יָד
[Holocaust memorial in Jerusalem]	Memorial and a Name	Yad va-Shem	יָד וָשֵׁם
The dot in the *vav* produces an "oo" sound	Judah (praising)	Y'hood-ah	יְהוּדָה
The dot on the top of the *vav* makes an "o" sound	day	yom	יוֹם
Look for the *nun sofit*	wine	ya-yin	יַיִן
No *dagesh* in the first letter, so a "k" sound, not "kh"	heavy	ka-ved	כָּבֵד
The 2nd *kav* has no *dagesh*, so it has a "kh" sound	star	ko-khav	כּוֹכָב

---

[10] Esther 2:16

Note	English	Transliteration	Hebrew
The *beit* at the end has no *dagesh*, so "v"	dog	ke-lev	כֶּלֶב
Notice *nun sofit*	cumin (spice)	kam-mon	כַּמּוֹן
Note the *kamats katan* produces an "o" sound	all, every	kol	כָּל
Note the use of the final letter	how	eykh	אֵיךְ
[Easy to read]	heart	lev	לֵב
Notice how this is a similar sounding word to *lev*, but uses a *vav* for "v"	Levi	Le-vee	לֵוִי
Note the *mem sofit*	bread	lekh-em	לֶחֶם
Notice the *nun sofit*	white, Laban	la-van	לָבָן
2nd vowel is under a silent letter	hundred	me-ah	מֵאָה
The dot in the *vav* gives an "oo" sound	flood	ma-bool	מַבּוּל
Without a dot the *vav* is a v sound	death	ma-vet	מָוֶת
Notice the *nun sofit*	from	min	מִן
[Simple word to read]	candle	ner	נֵר
[Easy word to read]	river	na-har	נָהָר
Note with the dot on the right the last letter is "sh"	snake	na-khash	נָחָשׁ

The dot above the *resh* indicates "o" sound		Nimrod	נִמְרֹד
[Familiar word!]	So be it, truly	Amen	אָמֵן
Kibboots vowel gives "oo" sound. *Samech* & *mem sofit* appear alike	ladder	soo-lam	סֻלָּם
Two "e" vowels read the same	book	sefer	סֵפֶר
[word from Psalms]	pause	selah	סֶלָה
Be careful with a *samech* at the end of a word, resembles a *mem sofit*	horse	soos	סוּס
Ayin is also a silent letter.[11]	until	ad	עַד
The *tseray* vowel here produce same sound as the *segol*	witness	ed	עֵד
As in the song *am Israel khie*, the people of Israel live	people	am	עַם
First "a" is sound slightly shortened	giant	an-ak	עֲנָק
The "o" sound is the dot above the *ayin*	Pharoah	Par-oh	פַּרְעֹה
Elkanah's 2nd wife, 1 Samuel 1:2	pearl or ruby	P'neen-nah	פְּנִנָּה

---

[11] Historically, it probably produced a more pronounced sound for the vowel underneath but in modern Hebrew there is no difference, unless perhaps the speaker is Sephardic Jewish

The "o" sound is a dot attached to the *peh* instead of to a *vav*	here	poh	פֹּה
Shv'h gives slight pause after the *peh*	fruit	p'ree	פְּרִי
Notice the *peh sofit* pronounced "f"	nose	af	אַף
No *dagesh* in middle letter so pronounced "v"	army	tsa-va	צָבָא
Notice the *nun sofit*	Zion	Tse-yon	צִיּוֹן
Uses the letter *tsa-dee sofit*	tree	ets	עֵץ
mem sofit	fast	tsom	צוֹם
[Easy to read]	voice	kol	קוֹל
Nun sofit	horn	keren	קֶרֶן
Tsadee sofit	summer	ka-yits	קַיִץ
[Easy to read]	flour	ke-makh	קֶמַח
The "r" sound is a throaty sound [12]	empty	rayk	רִיק
The "o" sound is the dot attached to the *aleph*	head	rosh	רֹאשׁ
Joshua 2:1	Rahab	Ra-khav	רָחָב
[Easy to read]	quarrel	reev	רִיב

---

[12] Put your hand on the front of your neck as you practise. It is different to an English "r" which is made using the lips.

Left-hand side dot, sin not a shin[13]	field	sa-deh	שָׂדֶה
Right-hand side, dot shin not a sin	peace	sha-lom	שָׁלוֹם
[Means "God heard"]	Samuel	Sh'moo-el	שְׁמוּאֵל
Notice the mem sofit	Song of Songs	Sheer ha-Sheer-im	שִׁיר הַשִׁירִים
Word uses mem and mem sofit	fault-free	ta-meem	תָּמִים
Note similar appearance of tav and khet	under	ta-khat	תַּחַת
"o" sound is short	Law	Tor-ah	תּוֹרָה
[Easy to read]	disciple	tal-meed	תַּלְמִיד

_____

[13] Sin is never right!

Lesson 3: Significance of the Hebrew letters

Each letter of the Hebrew alphabet represents a different picture. The chart below goes through each of the letters and gives the most well-known meanings. For example, the "b" sound is a picture of a house, and the name of the letter is *beit*, and this is much like the word for house, *bayit*. Again, the "g" sound, the *gimmel*, was used as a sign for a camel. Indeed, the Hebrew word for camel is *gamal*, which is very similar to the name of the letter. The "m" sound, the *mem*, represents water. The Hebrew word for water is *mayim*, which again reflects the name of the letter. The letter *ayin* is used as a pictogram for the eye. The Hebrew word for eye is also *ayin*. The same applies to the *peh*, which is also the word in Hebrew for mouth. Bear all this in mind as you go through the chart. The name of the letter may be similar to the word it stands for, or it may be the exact Hebrew word for it.

Now consider the personal name for God, pronounced *Ye-ho-vah*. It is a word which English speakers often refer to as *Jehovah* or *Yah-weh*. It is written in the Hebrew Bible *yod, hey, vav, hey*. Using the Hebrew letter pictures and going to each letter in turn from right to left, this cries out to us, "Hand, behold, nail, behold." It draws us to the image of the Son of God nailed to a Roman cross. I have shaded each relevant letter in the chart to make it easy to follow.

א	aleph	ox or first
ב	beit	house
ג	gimel	camel
ד	dalet	door
ה	hey	behold or take note
ו	vav	nail, peg, stick or hook
ז	zayin	spear, weapon
ח	khet	fence, thread
ט	tet	snake, surround
י	yod	hand
כ	kaph	palm
ל	lamed	learn

מ	mem	waters
נ	nun	continue/activity/ life/plant
ס	samekh	fish/prop/turn
ע	ayin	eye
פ	peh	mouth
צ	tsadee	fishhook
ק	kof	monkey
ר	reysh	head
שׁ	shin	tooth
ת	tav	sign, mark

Jesus prayed in John 12:28, "Father, glorify Your name." Then we read the following: "a voice came from heaven, *saying*, 'I have both glorified *it* and will glorify *it* again.'" Indeed, the name of God is glorified by the image of beholding (or taking note of) the hand of the One pierced by a nail on the Cross, dying for our sins.

In Revelation 22:13, written in Greek, Jesus says "I am the Alpha and the Omega, the Beginning and the End, the First and the Last." Now to the Hebrew mind, this is the equivalent of Jesus saying that He is the *Aleph* and the *Tav*, since these are the first and last letters of the Hebrew alphabet. The *aleph* represents the position of being first. The *tav* speaks of the sign or mark of the nail. *Tav* used to be written as a cross in ancient script, which is most interesting, given that in Scripture, those loyal to the Lord are marked by Him as His, in contrast to the Mark of the Beast which will denote belonging to the Antichrist.[14] The English word "alphabet" is derived from the first two words of the Greek alphabet, "alpha" and "beta." The Hebrew word for alphabet is *aleph-beit*.

Jesus tells us in Matthew 5:18, "For assuredly, I say to you, till heaven and earth pass away, one jot or one tittle will by no means pass from the law till all is fulfilled." The "jot" is the translation of the letter *yod*, which is the smallest Hebrew letter. The "tittle" is the *kots*, which is the miniscule stroke or flourish added to some letters, including the tiny *yod*. An example of the importance of this tiny stroke is when you look back at the alphabet chart, what distinguishes the *dalet* from the *resh* is the addition of a *kots*.

---

[14] Ezekiel 9:4, Revelation 13:16

We must not assume that the use of the names of the letters always reflects this pictogram model. You may, for example, be familiar with the name of the Israeli intelligence organisation, the *Shin Beit*, and this is simply an acronym[15] drawn from the initials of its title in Hebrew, the "General Security Service."

A most charming use of initials which I encountered is the first name of one of my online Hebrew teachers, Nili. Her name is an acronym of the verse, "the Strength of Israel will not lie."[16] I have emphasised the initial letters in the phrase to show you how the name has been compiled. The transliteration of the verse reads: *nets-akh yis-ra-el lo y'shak-ker*

נֵצַח יִשְׂרָאֵל לֹא יְשַׁקֵּר

---

[15] Abbreviation from initial letters of a word, like USA for United States of America.
[16] 1 Samuel 15:29

Lesson 4: Names for God in the New Testament

We do not directly see the personal name of God, Yehovah, in the New Testament. We must ask ourselves, when the Greek text refers to "kurios" (Lord), if this is a reference to Yehovah. Take, for example, Mark 1:3, "The voice of one crying in the wilderness: 'Prepare the way of the LORD; Make His paths straight.'" This is a quotation from Isaiah 40:3. We know from the Hebrew text of this verse in Isaiah that it is indeed the word *Yehovah* being referred to. We get a similar picture by looking at Mark 11:9: "Then those who went before and those who followed cried out, saying: Hosanna! 'Blessed *is* He who comes in the name of the LORD!'" This is a reference to Psalm 118:26, which includes the name of God, Yehovah, "Blessed is he who comes in the name of the LORD."[17]

"The Lord of Sabaoth" is a term used twice in the New Testament and there "Lord" means Yehovah. The first occurrence is when the Apostle Paul quotes Isaiah: "And as Isaiah said before: "unless the LORD of Sabaoth had left us a seed…" "[18] This is a reference to the name for God used in the Old Testament in various places.[19] The second reference in the New Testament is in James 5:4: "Indeed the wages of the laborers who mowed your fields, which you kept back by fraud, cry out; and the cries of the reapers have reached the ears of the Lord of Sabaoth."

Many casual readers of the New Testament who come across the term "The LORD (or Lord) of Sabaoth," tend to inaccurately assume that this is a reference to God being the

---

[17] Other examples are Matthew 4:4 (Deuteronomy 8:3), Matthew 4:7 (Deuteronomy 6:16), Matthew 4:10 (Deuteronomy 6:13), Luke 13:35 (Psalm 118:26).
[18] Romans 9:29
[19] Such as Isaiah 1:9.

Lord of the Sabbath. However, it is a reference to the Old Testament title for God, "The LORD of the hosts of heaven's armies," or "Yehovah of armies." This is sometimes translated, "the Lord of hosts." We are taught in Revelation 19:13,14 that, in the vision given to John about the return of the Lord Jesus, "the armies in heaven, clothed in fine linen, white and clean, followed Him on white horses." It is said that this name for God occurs 235 times in the Bible.[20] The warning to unrighteous employers comes across far more strongly when we appreciate that they will soon face the Lord of Heaven's armies.

I have put the words in the chart which are relevant to this New Testament term, "Lord of Sabaoth." I have also included the word for Sabbath. The reason for this is to indicate that although there is an apparent similarity in English, the Hebrew shows us clearly that they are completely different words. You will also see there the modern Hebrew word for army as well as for the "Israel Defence Force." Interestingly, Jesus also tells us that He is "Lord of the Sabbath."[21]

Another name for God which we particularly associate with the New Testament is "Father." The term "*Abba* Father" is used three times in the New Testament. We have Mark 14:36, "And He said, "Abba, Father, all things *are* possible for You. Take this cup away from Me; nevertheless, not what I will, but what You *will*." " Then Romans 8:15, "For you did not receive the spirit of bondage again to fear, but you received the Spirit of adoption by whom we cry out, "Abba, Father." " Finally, Galatians 4:6, "And because you are sons, God has sent forth the Spirit of His Son into your hearts, crying out, "Abba, Father! " " When we visit the land of Israel, it is such

[20]"One for Israel" internet article "What does the Lord of Hosts mean?" accessed 7th May 2022.
[21] Matthew 12:8, Mark 2:28, Luke 6:5

a joy to hear the young children cry out, *Abba*. We naturally assume it is the Hebrew word for Daddy. In fact, it is an Aramaic word firmly fixed in modern Hebrew and closely related to the Hebrew word for father.

When the disciples asked the Lord Jesus to teach them to pray, He answered that the prayer should be addressed to "Our Father, who is in heaven…"[22] In modern Hebrew "our Father" is *aveenoo*. *Av* is the word for father, and there is a suffix *eenoo* meaning "our."

It is the same story for the Hebrew word "mother" and the family term, *ima*. The latter is also of Aramaic origin and is used for Mummy. The two words are included in the chart for this lesson.

In looking at the subject of this lesson on names for God, it is important to remember that the name *Yehovah* is considered by Jewish people to be too holy to pronounce. For this reason, just as our Bibles may well translate the word as "Lord," so Hebrew readers will generally read out the word as *Adonai*, meaning "Lord," when they see the letters *yod, hey, vav, hey*.

Robert's comments

Five thousand times in the Hebrew Bible, God's personal name – Yehovah – appears in the text. When the Jewish community in Alexandria (in Egypt) organised a translation of the Hebrew Bible into Greek, the Septuagint's (LXX) translators used Kurios (LORD) in the Greek for Yehovah. The Pentateuch (first five books of the Bible) was translated in the mid-3rd century BC, and the remainder was ready by 132 BC.

---

[22] Matthew 6:9

Translations into English and other languages have nearly all followed what became a tradition of printing LORD (in block letters) for Yehovah. It is no exaggeration to say that Jewish people have a superstition of saying the name Yehovah. It is only openly said once a year, by the Cohanim (priests) during Yom Kippur (Day of Atonement) services in synagogues.

The question arises, is it right not to use the name Yehovah? In the Ten Commandments, we find this stated: "You shall not take the name of the LORD your God in vain, for the LORD will not hold him guiltless who takes His name in vain."[23] The word LORD stands in place of Yehovah. Leviticus 24:11 provides an example of where a man blasphemed the name of Yehovah and cursed. The judgement of God was for Israel to stone him. There is no restriction on saying the name Yehovah, which – as God's personal name – must always be honoured. Therefore, the Jewish community should not be restricted in using the name. The command is not to use the personal name of God lightly, *in vain*.

---

[23] Exodus 20:7

English	Transliteration	Hebrew
The Lord of Hosts	Ye-ho-vah Ts-va-ot	יְהֹוָה צְבָאוֹת
army (singular)	ts-va	צְבָא
Israel	Yis-ra-el	יִשְׂרָאֵל
Israel Defence Force (IDF)	Ts-va ha-Haganah l'Yisrael	צְבָא הַהֲגָנָה לְיִשְׂרָאֵל
Sabbath	Shab-bat	שַׁבָּת
father (Hebrew)	av	אָב
daddy (Aramaic)	ab-ba	אַבָּא
Avram (exalted father)	Av-ram	אַבְרָם
Abraham (father of a multitude)	Av-ra-ham	אַבְרָהָם
our Father	Av-ee-noo	אָבִינוּ
mother (Hebrew)	em	אֵם
mummy (Aramaic origin)	ima	אִמָּא
Lord	Adonai	אֲדֹנָי

Lesson 5: Jesus Christ, the Son of Man

We are now going to look at the exalted name of Jesus. We are told "that at the name of Jesus every knee should bow, of those in heaven, and of those on earth, and of those under the earth." [24]

Many readers will already be familiar with the Hebrew name of Jesus, Yeshua, which the angel gave to Joseph in a dream for the Child to be born to his betrothed: "you shall call His name JESUS, for He will save His people from their sins."[25]

The name Yeshua written in Hebrew appears in this lesson's chart. Now that you know its Hebrew anglicised form, you should be able to spot it in your Old Testament reading, particularly in the books of Ezra and Nehemiah. [26] It may well be written as "Jeshua," as the *yod* is sometimes translated as a "j." There is no "j" in modern Hebrew, and the jury is still out as to whether that sound existed in ancient Hebrew.

A Hebrew reader going through the Old Testament will spot the essence of the name Yeshua when they read the word for salvation or deliverance. There may well be minor grammatical changes according to context, but the underlying word will be clear. Examples of such verses are listed in the footnote below.[27] If you are interested, you can use an online Bible such as BibleHub.com and look up the verse in English containing the word for salvation and then go to the Hebrew page and

---

[24] Philippians 2:10
[25] Matthew 1:21
[26]Verses include Ezra 2:2, 2:36, 3:2,3:8,9, 4:3, 5:2, 8:33 and Nehemiah 7:39, 9:4,5, 10:9, 11:26, 12:8,24
[27]Exodus 15:2, Psalm27:1 , Isaiah 12:2, 61:10

spot *Yeshuah*. One example is Isaiah 12:2 which says, "Behold, God *is* my salvation, I will trust and not be afraid; 'For YAH, the LORD, *is* my strength and song; He also has become my salvation." If you study the last word translated "my salvation," the Hebrew letters spell out the word *li-yeshuah*, with the *li* being a prefix indicating possession of the salvation, the *yeshuah*. We can see from the chart that the Hebrew word for salvation has an extra letter at the end, a *hey*, and this "h" sound can be heard, making it a distinctly different word to the name *Yeshua*, and yet inextricably bound with it. If you read out the verse in English quoted above from Isaiah and on the two occasions the word salvation appears, replace it with the Hebrew word *yeshuah*, and then all will become clear!

A further example of a variant of *yeshuah* in the Hebrew Bible is in Genesis 49:18. Here, dying Jacob provides blessings and judgements concerning the tribes of Israel. He closes the piece about Dan with "I have waited for your salvation, O Lord!" Now when we read from the New Testament, we may see in a new light aged Simeon holding Jesus as a baby saying, "For my eyes have seen Your salvation."[28]

Now we are going on to consider His office, "Christ." This is the Greek word for Messiah or Anointed One. If you examine the Hebrew spelling of this word in the chart (*Masheeakh*), it follows an obscure Hebrew grammatical rule. Logic would suggest that the last sound in the word should be the vowel (*patakh*) under the final letter, here a *khet*. However, the vowel at the end of a word under a *khet* is read before the letter. The same rule applies if this vowel falls under a final letter of a word which is an *ayin* or a *hey* with a *dagesh* (dot) in. The

---

[28] Luke 2:30

grammatical term for this is a *furtive patakh*. Jesus used the root letters from this word *Masheeakh*, when He stood in the synagogue, and read from Isaiah the proclamation, "The Spirit of the LORD *is* upon Me, because He has **anointed** Me to preach the gospel to *the* poor."[29] You can see the exact Hebrew wording in the chart.

Jesus is referred to as "the Son of Man" over 80 times in the New Testament, and this title is used by Him to refer to Himself more than any other. Aspects of this can be rather puzzling. Ezekiel the prophet is called "son of man" over 90 times. In that context it simply denotes a human being. If an Israeli wants to convey that he is merely flesh and blood, he may well say, *ani ben adam!* This literally means, "I am a son of Adam." Adam is very close to the Hebrew word for red and was so named because God formed him from the ground (probably red), the *adamah*. Esau was called *Edom* (also meaning red) because he ate the red pottage.[30] Adam is also very close to the Hebrew word for blood, *dam*.

We see in the Gospels that Jesus referred to Himself as the Son of Man coming with, or on, the clouds.[31] The reaction of the High Priest upon hearing this was that he "tore his clothes, saying, "He has spoken blasphemy!" " The reason for such a strong reaction is that this was an obvious reference to the Son of Man coming on the clouds, that "all peoples, nations, and languages should serve Him" in the Messianic vision granted to Daniel.[32] Most of the Old Testament was written in Hebrew, hence Ezekiel is referred to as *Ben Adam*. However, a

---

[29] Luke 4:18
[30] Genesis 25:30
[31] Mark 14:62, Matthew 26:64.
[32] Daniel 7:13,14

tiny proportion of it was written in Aramaic. Some sections of the book of Ezra were written in Aramaic as well as Daniel 2:4 to 7:28.[33] Hence, the Messianic verse in Daniel 7:13 about Him coming on the clouds was originally written in Aramaic. There, the Messiah is described as *Bar Enash* rather than *Ben Adam*. Clearly, Jesus was claiming to the High Priest to be the Promised One from Daniel 7:13 coming on the clouds.

You will probably recognise the Aramaic word for son from the term *Bar Mitzvah*,[34] or "son of the commandment," which is the name given to the ceremony of reading the law when a boy reaches the age of 13 and is said to come under the authority of the law of Moses.

For the purposes of our lesson, we will consider the plural of the Hebrew words for son and daughter: *ben* and *bat*. Neither word follows the exact rule for forming plurals. *Ben* then becomes *baneem* and *bat* becomes *banot*. We see from these two words how the vowel sounds in the singular are changed to form the plural. A further example of plural formation with changed vowels is the word for stone shown in the chart. This is of significance because it is a feminine word, yet it takes a typically male plural ending of *yod, mem*. It remains feminine, so any adjective will also be feminine. There are a number of this sort of irregular plural formations in Hebrew.

The word *mitzvah* is interesting too. You can see the *vav* (which so often expresses an "o" or "oo" sound) being used as a consonant. The word is feminine, so the plural ending is typically *ot*. Although, strictly speaking, *mitzvah* means

---

[33] Also Jeremiah 10:11 and within Genesis 31:47 – Franz Rosenthal "A Grammar of Biblical Aramaic."

[34] This has been anglicised as though it has a *zayin* in, the same for the word *Kibbutz*

commandment, the word is used by Jewish people to refer to a good deed such as donating to charity or helping an elderly person cross the road. There is the usual religious spirit in Judaism and lack of assurance of salvation, and this is expressed through attempting to live the sort of life where the good deeds outweigh the bad deeds.

Matthew writes, "Behold, the virgin shall be with child, and bear a Son, and they shall call His name Immanuel," which is translated, "God with us." "[35] If we break down the Hebrew components of this name, we get *im* meaning "with," then *anu* which is "us" and finally *El*, the word for "God" or "god."

A more obscure reference to the coming Messiah occurs in Genesis 49:10: "The scepter will not depart from Judah, nor the staff from between his feet, until Shiloh comes and the allegiance of the nations is his."[36] Shiloh is thought to refer to the Messiah as the Peaceful One, and is related to the word *shalom*. An apt term indeed for the One who said, "Peace I leave with you, My peace I give to you; not as the world gives do I give to you. Let not your heart be troubled, neither let it be afraid." [37]

Robert's comments

Many people are familiar with the fact that Jewish boys have a ceremony named *Bar Mitzvah* (literally, Son of a Commandment). This is a well-established tradition, particularly in the Orthodox world, and Jewish boys at 13 take part in a ceremony

---

[35] Matthew 1:23
[36] American spelling retained due to copyright
[37] John 14:27

in synagogue, being regarded as adults with religious responsibilities. Interestingly, there is no commandment in the Hebrew Bible that is connected to the tradition. The first record of a Bar Mitzvah goes back only to the 13th century in France, when a father stated that he was no longer responsible for his 13-year-old son; and there was a ceremony.

The Bar Mitzvah introduces the assumption that the boy is now an adult, and therefore will wear phylacteries (small boxes containing Scripture from Moses strapped onto the forehead and left arm) for prayer time, and join the minyan (quorum) of at least 10 men for public prayers. But what does the word of God suggest to the reader as being the sort of age when a young man reaches an age of responsibility, acting as an adult? Taking several Old Testament passages together,[38] it seems obvious that 20 is regarded biblically as the age of early adult responsibility.

Clearly, Bar Mitzvah did not exist in Biblical times, and any idea that Jesus had one has no foundation. Some people think that young Jesus, aged 12, went up to Jerusalem for an early form of Bar Mitzvah. The relevant portion of Scripture[39] shows that Jesus and His earthly family went up to the capital city to celebrate the pilgrim festival of Passover.

---

[38] Exodus 30:11-16, Numbers 1:1-3, Numbers 26:1-4
[39] Luke 2:41-52

47

English	Transliteration	Hebrew
Joshua (Yehovah is salvation)	Ye-hosh-ua	יְהוֹשֻׁעַ
alternative spelling	Ye-hosh-ua	יְהוֹשׁוּעַ
Jesus [short for Yehoshua]	Ye-shua	יֵשׁוּעַ
Hoshea [original name of Joshua]	Ho-shea	הוֹשֵׁעַ
Salvation, deliverance	Ye-shuah	יְשׁוּעָה
Messiah	Ma-shee-akh	מָשִׁיחַ
Jehovah has anointed Me (Isaiah 61:1)	ma-shakh Ye-ho-vah Otee	מָשַׁח יְהוָה אֹתִי
Adam	Ad-am	אָדָם
Son of Man (Hebrew)	Ben Ad-am	בֶּן־אָדָם
Son of Man (Aramaic)	Bar En-ash	בַּר אֱנָשׁ
earth	a-dam-ah	אֲדָמָה
red	a-dom	אָדֹם
Edom	E-dom	אֱדוֹם
blood	dam	דָּם
Bar Mitzvah	Bar Mits-vah	בַּר מִצְוָה
Bat Mitzvah	Bat Mits-vah	בַּת מִצְוָה
sons	ban-im	בָּנִים
daughters	ban-ot	בָּנוֹת

stone (f)	ev-en	אֶבֶן
stones (pl)	ava-neem	אֲבָנִים
commandments	mits-vot	מִצְוֹת
with	eem	עִם
us	a-noo	אָנוּ
God or god	El	אֵל
Emmanuel	Im-man-oo-el	עִמָּנוּ אֵל
Shiloh	Shee-loh	שִׁילֹה

Lesson 6: Titles for Jesus & the Jewish calendar

We are now examining some of the titles of Jesus in the New Testament. These terms have special relevance in the Jewish world, and we can see this because of the association with present-day Jewish festivals, prayers, and practices.

The One born in Bethlehem (House of Bread) referred to Himself as the bread of life. Bread is the most obvious staple food. It was so in Biblical times, and we understand the claim; Jesus said that He is the One upon whom we need to be utterly dependent. The modern-day blessing recited each Sabbath and at religious feasts by Jewish people to bless the bread of the meal is as follows:

בָּרוּךְ אַתָּה אֲדֹנָי אֱלֹהֵינוּ מֶלֶךְ הָעוֹלָם הַמּוֹצִיא
לֶחֶם מִן הָאָרֶץ

The transliteration is: *Barukh atah Adonai Elohaynoo melekh ha-olam ha-motsee lekhem min ha-arets.* The translation is "Blessed are You, Lord our God, King of the Universe, who brings forth bread from the earth." I have put the word for "the earth" in the chart, and this is also a term used for the Land of Israel. There is a newspaper in Israel called *Ha Aretz.*

At Passover, the bread is unleavened and usually has a striped appearance, with little holes in, so that it is pierced bread. It is called *matzah* and we can see the symbolism of the One by whose stripes we are healed and who was pierced for our transgressions.[40] When Jesus was scourged, a Roman bodyguard called a lictor (or two working alternately) would have

---

[40] Isaiah 53:5

lashed Him with a whip containing metal and bone, which would deliberately cut into the back, forming stripes of wounds, with flesh falling away. At what we now call the Last Supper (a Passover meal which Jesus adapted to introduce the New Covenant), and while they were eating, Jesus took bread, blessed and broke *it,* and gave *it* to the disciples and said, "Take, eat; this is My body."[41] If you are not familiar with matzah, it closely resembles a water biscuit or a crispbread. When you break it, it snaps in a way that regular bread fails to do.

Matzah is rightly regarded in the Jewish world as perfect bread. It contains no leaven – which is a picture of sinfulness so often in the word of God. Its only ingredients are the finest flour and water from a fresh, unpolluted flowing stream. It is baked in a fierce oven. The pure ingredients and the baking procedure picture the Lord in His sinless nature and His unique suffering. There is an additional blessing said at Passover over the matzah:

בָּרוּךְ אַתָּה אֲדֹנָי אֱלֹהֵינוּ מֶלֶךְ הָעוֹלָם
אֲשֶׁר קִדְּשָׁנוּ בְּמִצְוֹתָיו וְצִוָּנוּ עַל אֲכִילַת מַצָּה

The transliteration reads, *Barukh atah Adonai Elohaynoo melekh ha-olam asher kidd-e sha-noo b'mitsotav v-tsoo-va-noo al akheeylat matsah.* This translates as, "Blessed are you, Lord our God, King of the Universe, who has sanctified us with His commandments and commanded us on the eating of matzah." Paul writes in his comments against immorality: "Do you not know that a little leaven leavens the whole lump? Therefore purge out the old leaven, that you may be a new lump, since you truly are unleavened. For indeed Christ, our Passover, was sacrificed

---

[41] Matthew 26:26

for us. Therefore let us keep the feast, not with old leaven, nor with the leaven of malice and wickedness, but with the unleavened bread of sincerity and truth."[42]

Jesus said, "I am the vine, you *are* the branches."[43] You may recognise the word for vine from the Hebrew blessing over wine used at festivals and the Sabbath meal, which is as follows:

$$\text{בָּרוּךְ אַתָּה אֲדֹנָי אֱלֹהֵינוּ מֶלֶךְ הָעוֹלָם בּוֹרֵא}$$
$$\text{פְּרִי הַגָּפֶן}$$

This reads, *Barookh atah Adonai Elohavynoo melekh ha-olam borey p'ree hagafen.* The meaning is, "Blessed are You, Lord our God, King of the Universe, who creates the fruit of the vine."

We go on to look at the word for light, *or* in the phrase "Light of the World." The Hebrew word for candlestick or lampstand, *menorah*, is a noun derived from the word *or*. As you examine *menorah* in the chart, you can see that *or* is contained within it. There are two main types of candelabra which you are likely to encounter in the Jewish world. The first is referred to as a *menorah* and it forms part of the emblem of Israel. It has a total of seven branches and is modelled on the huge lampstand at the Temple in Jerusalem.[44] The candelabrum used at the Feast of Dedication has a similar appearance but it has a total of nine branches. *Khanukah* is not a Biblical festival. However, it honours the re-dedication of the Temple when the Maccabean fighters beat Antiochus Epiphanes and the

---

[42] 1 Corinthians 5:6-8
[43] John 15:5
[44] Exodus 25:31-40

Syrian Greeks. Children love *Khanukah*[45] because the candle in the middle is used on the first day of the festival to light one candle, then two on the second day, until on the eighth day all nine candles are alight. It is also becoming popular to give gifts to the children on each night of the festival. Since *Khanukah* falls usually during the month of December, this is much appreciated by those who feel left out of the Christmas celebrations because of being Jewish.

Before the Shabbat Friday evening meal, the lady of the house lights a pair of candles and recites the special blessing:

בָּרוּךְ אַתָּה אֲדֹנָי אֱלֹהֵינוּ מֶלֶךְ הָעוֹלָם אֲשֶׁר קִדְּשָׁנוּ בְּמִצְוֹתָיו וְצִוָּנוּ לְהַדְלִיק נֵר שֶׁל שַׁבָּת

Barookh atah Adonai Elohavynoo melekh ha-olam asher kide-sha-noo b'mits-otav v'tsi-va-noo l'hadleek ner shel shabbat. The translation being, "Blessed are You, Lord our God, King of the universe, who has sanctified us with His commandments, and commanded us to kindle the light of Shabbat." This is interesting as, in fact, there is no such commandment in the Bible to light the Sabbath candles.

Jesus said, "I am the way, the truth, and the life," and the words for these terms are in the chart. The word for "way" is an irregular feminine noun. Yet it takes the typical male plural. I have illustrated this with the phrase "good ways," with the adjective being feminine plural. The word for "truth" is *emet*. In the chart, under *emet* I have put the name *Amit-tie*, the father

---

[45] Usually spelt Chanukah but in this book I have used a "K" for the first letter to remind the reader that the word will not sound like the beginning of the word "cherry." Remember that the *khet* has a throaty sound like the last sound of the word "loch."

of the prophet Jonah.[46] This name is variously translated: truth, God's truth, and my truth. You may recognise the word for life from the Jewish toast to life, *LeChaim*.[47] It is also a boy's name, as in Israel's first president, Chaim Weizmann. You also see jewellery pendants with the first two letters of the word, *khet* and *yod*.

"I am the door of the sheep…I am the door. If anyone enters by Me, he will be saved, and will go in and out and find pasture."[48] This is a most touching allusion, since in biblical times the sheep would be protected at night in a stone enclosure with a gap for them to enter and come out the following morning. The shepherd would sleep across this gap to protect the sheep and keep them where they should be. He was literally the door. There is a Jewish blessing associated with doors. You may be familiar with the *mezuzah* fixed to the Jewish doorway in accordance with Deuteronomy 6:4-8: "Hear, O Israel: the Lord our God, the Lord is one! You shall love the Lord your God with all your heart, with all your soul, and with all your strength. And these words which I command you today shall be in your heart…**You shall write them on the doorposts of your house** and on your gates." The first part of that extract is known as the *Sh'ma* and is included in the two passages from Deuteronomy inscribed on the tiny parchment inside the outer casing of the *mezuzah*. Jesus describes this exhortation to whole-heartedly love God as "… *the* first and great commandment."[49] We will now go on to look at the blessing for Jewish people to recite while attaching the *mezuzah* to the doorpost.

---

[46] 2 Kings 14:25, Jonah 1:1
[47] Following the pronunciation guidelines in this book, it would be *LeKhaim*.
[48] John 10:7-9
[49] Matthew 22:38

בָּרוּךְ אַתָּה אֲדֹנָי אֱלֹהֵינוּ מֶלֶךְ הָעוֹלָם אֲשֶׁר
קִדְּשָׁנוּ בְּמִצְוֹתָיו וְצִוָּנוּ לִקְבּוֹעַ מְזוּזָה

Barookh atah Adonai Elo-hay-noo melekh ha-olam asher kide-sha-noo b'mits-otav v'tsivanoo lik-boya m'zooz-ah. The meaning is "Blessed are You Lord our God, King of the Universe who sanctified us with His commandments and commanded us to affix a mezuzah." The word *mezuzah* means "doorpost" as well as the small box attached to it containing the passage.

"I am the good shepherd. The good shepherd gives His life for the sheep."[50] Amazingly, Jesus is not only the shepherd to protect the sheep, but He is also "The Lamb of God who takes away the sin of the world!"[51] The writer to the Hebrews describes Jesus as our great High Priest.[52] We know that He is both our High Priest and the sacrifice offered by him on the Day of Atonement, the only day in the year when he is permitted to enter the inner part of the Temple, the Holy of Holies. "But into the second part the high priest *went* alone once a year, not without blood, which he offered for himself and *for* the people's sins *committed* in ignorance."[53] This brings us to consider the Day of Atonement, Yom Kippur. Nowadays, in the synagogue a series of prayers is recited regarding confession of sin. The *al khet* is repeated 10 times in the service that day. It is a confession of many types of sin (*khet*) such as sins of speech, and the prayer includes a plea for God's forgiveness.

---

[50] John 10:11
[51] John 1:29
[52] Hebrews 4:14
[53] Hebrews 9:7

Robert's comments

Concerning Chanukah,[54] the revolt led by Yehuda HaMakabi
(Judah the Hammer) was the world's first deliverance by a
guerrilla group against a great enemy, by 164 BC. This seems
to be honoured in the Book of Hebrews, speaking of those
who through faith, "subdued kingdoms, worked righteousness, obtained promises, stopped the mouths of lions,
quenched the violence of fire, escaped the edge of the sword,
out of weakness were made strong, became valiant in battle,
turned to flight the armies of the aliens."[55] Even more significantly, John's Gospel account includes this, "Now it was the
Feast of Dedication in Jerusalem, and it was winter. And Jesus
walked in the temple, in Solomon's porch."[56] So the Lord was
there in the capital city during Chanukah, and John's mention
of this confirms His approval of its remembrance of heroism.
The central lamp of the *Chanukiah* (*Shamash*) is used to light
the eight other lamps, supposedly to recall the finding of oil
that kept the Temple lamp lit for eight days. This is a myth,
based on a late story, being put into writing in the Talmud 600
years later. The real miracle was the Lord enabling the Macca-
beans to defeat the enemy and re-dedicate the Temple. The
Lord was silent for 400 years, from the time of the prophet
Malachi until the events connected to the birth of John the
Baptist.

Having the *mezuzah* on the doorpost is regarded as extremely important to religious Jews. In the 19th century, Theo-
dore Herzl was seeking to provide a haven for Europe's Jews

---

[54] Usual spelling but in the Hebrew lessons in this book it is spelt *Khanukah*. You may
also see it written as *Hanukkah*.
[55] Hebrews 11:33,34
[56] John 10:22,23

to escape from deep-seated anti-Jewishness. He was opposed in his Zionist aims by many European rabbis, Orthodox and Liberal. Some of the Orthodox maintained that the presence of a mezuzah on the doorposts of Jewish homes was sufficient to provide divine protection from the destroyer.[57] Sadly, this was a false hope and all the religious Jews liquidated in the Holocaust (*Shoah* in Hebrew, the word for "destruction"), would have fitted mezuzahs at home.

---

[57] For further understanding of this belief, see the internet article on Chabad.org entitled "The Protective Power of the Mezuzah."

English	Transliteration	Hebrew
blessed are you	barookh atah	בָּרוּךְ אַתָּה
Universe or World	ol-am	עוֹלָם
bread	lekh-em	לֶחֶם
the earth, Israel	ha-arets	הָאָרֶץ
Bread of Life	Lekh-em Ha- Kha-yim	לֶחֶם הַחַיִּים
unleavened bread	mats-ah	מַצָּה
I (am)	anokhee	אָנֹכִי
the (prefix)	ha	הַ
world	o-lam	עוֹלָם
Light of the World	Or Ha-O-lam	אוֹר הָעוֹלָם
candlestick, lampstand	m'nor-ah	מְנוֹרָה
Khanukah lamp (nine branches)	Kha-noo-kiah	חֲנֻכִּיָּה
servant [lamp]	sham-mash	שַׁמָּשׁ
candle	ner	נֵר
The Vine	Ha-Gef-en	הַגֶּפֶן
The Way	Ha-Derekh	הַדֶּרֶךְ

good ways	dra-khim to-vot	דְּרָכִים טוֹבוֹת
The Truth	Ha-Emet	הָאֱמֶת
Amittai	Amit-tai	אֲמִתַּי
The Life	Ha-Kha-yim	הַחַיִּים
door	de-let	דֶּלֶת
mezuzah	m'zooz-ah	מְזוּזָה
shepherd, pastor	ro-eh	רוֹעֶה
good	tov	טוֹב
The Good Shepherd	Ha-Ro-eh Ha-Tov	הָרוֹעֶה הַטּוֹב
The High Priest	Ha-Co-hen Ha-Gadol	הַכּוֹהֵן הַגָּדוֹל
The Lamb of God	Seh Ha-Elo-heem	שֵׂה הָאֱלֹהִים
the sin of the world	kha-tat ha-olam	חַטַּאת הָעוֹלָם
for the sin	al khet	עַל חֵטְא

Lesson 7: The Holy Spirit

We are now turning our attention to the third Person of the Godhead. In Hebrew, this is *Ruakh HaKodesh*. The first word is used for either spirit or wind. This is interesting in the light of what Jesus says in John 3:8, "The wind blows where it wishes, and you hear the sound of it, but cannot tell where it comes from and where it goes. So is everyone who is born of the Spirit."

The definite article *ha* is added as a prefix to the word holy, so that it reads *HaKodesh*. Normally, for the "o" sound there would be a *vav* with a dot above it after the *kof*. Sometimes, however, like here, the *vav* is dispensed with, leaving just the dot above the letter *kof*. The word for holy (*kodesh*) beautifully illustrates one of the main grammatical structures of the Hebrew language. That is the use of root letters, usually three. So, with the word for holy the root letters are clearly *kof, dalet* and *shin*. I will put the terms in the chart for related words in Hebrew so that you can spot the three root letters as you seek to read them. You can see the word for the Temple as *Beit HaMikdash*, which literally means "the house of holiness or sanctity." In the Lord's prayer, Jesus teaches us to pray "Hallowed be Your name," and the first word, "Hallowed," is shown in the chart in Hebrew for you to spot the three root letters. We see the same word in the Hebrew/Aramaic prayer of mourning called the Kaddish. The meaning is "Your great name be magnified and hallowed or sanctified" and reads as follows (*yitgadal v'yitkad-dash sh'meh rab-bah*):

יִתְגַּדַּל וְיִתְקַדַּשׁ שְׁמֵהּ רַבָּא

We are now ready for a complete phrase in Hebrew from the Old Testament. Isaiah 6:3 is included in the chart for you to read. All three words in this verse have been covered in our studies together!

We will take another example of the three root letters, this time in modern spoken Hebrew. The root letters are taken from the masculine singular past tense of the verb. We will illustrate the concept using the sentence "He **wrote** a **letter** and put the **address** on the envelope." In English the three words in bold type sound and appear very different. They each feature in Hebrew in the chart where the root letters are easy to spot; they derive from the word "wrote." In the word for "letter" a *mem* is typically placed at the beginning of the root letters to form the noun, making the word *mictav*. A letter is something we write! We need to put the address on the envelope and the Hebrew word for "address" is *c'tovet* and here a letter *tav* is added at the end of the word to form the noun.

A further example is related to the word for healing. You may have heard the Hebrew term for God, *Yehovah Rafa*,[58] meaning "the Lord who heals." We can see the three root letters there for healing, *resh*, *fey* and *aleph*. In the chart I have put various associated terms, from which you can clearly follow the use of the three letters belonging to the root. If you examine the term for "complete healing" in the chart, note how the word for peace, shalom, is used as a feminine adjective. Shalom also means complete or paid in full.

There are over 90 verses in the New Testament concerning the Holy Spirit, and the reader may well be wondering how frequently He is mentioned in the Old Testament. The answer

---

[58] Adapted from Exodus 15:26

is that the He is rarely directly referred to in those terms. I have included extracts from Psalm 51:11 and Isaiah 63:10[59] in the chart.

There are many verses referring to the Spirit of the Lord in the Old Testament. Jesus read one of these, Isaiah 61:1, in the synagogue in Nazareth, "The Spirit of the Lord GOD *is* upon Me, because the LORD has anointed Me to preach good tidings to the poor..."[60] In light of our earlier lesson, it is noteworthy that the Scripture uses both terms for God next to one another: Adonai (Lord) and Yehovah.

Consideration of God's holiness brings us to Hebrew ways of expressing superlatives. In English we may say "the best of times." In Hebrew this would be expressed as the "time of times." We have Biblical examples of this in the chart, as in the case of the "Song of Songs," which is the Hebrew name for the "Song of Solomon," and these are the first two words of the book. Another example relevant to this lesson is the special part of the Temple called "The Holy of Holies."[61] In English we would refer to this as the "most holy place." Then we have the title "King of kings" used of the Lord Jesus.[62] You can see this term in the Old Testament, speaking of Nebuchadnezzar, King of Babylon, and Artaxerxes, King of Persia.[63]

When we pray, we may wish to praise God for His immeasurable holiness, and address Him as "the indescribably, supremely Holy One." In Hebrew, we read in Isaiah concerning the response of the *seraphim*, "And one cried to another

[59] See also Isaiah 63:11
[60] Luke 4:18
[61] Exodus 26:33
[62] Revelation 17:14 (Hebrew spelling in chart)
[63] Ezekiel 26:7, Ezra 7:12

and said: "Holy, holy, holy *is* the LORD of hosts; The whole earth *is* full of His glory!" "[64] We see this term repeated by the four living creatures around the throne of God in the New Testament.[65] Jeremiah also repeats the word "earth" three times for greater emphasis to his message: "O earth, earth, earth, Hear the word of the LORD!"[66] In the New Testament, this idea of a threefold repetition for emphasis is indicated in Peter's vision of impure or unclean animals, "This was done three times. And the object was taken up into heaven again."[67] This Hebrew pattern of repetition for emphasis contrasts with English, whereby repetition is usually regarded as tautology — unnecessary use of words.

The word for seraphs is in the chart and you will now be able to recognise clearly from the Hebrew that this is a plural word, so there is no place for writing in English "seraphims." The same applies to the term *cherubim*, which I have seen online as "cherubims!"

Robert's comments

Although the Holy Spirit is mentioned in the Hebrew Bible a number of times, often as "The Spirit" and "the Spirit of God," the Jewish world does not have the same view as Christians about Him. Religious Jews are familiar with the Hebrew wording (*Ruakh Ha Kodesh*) yet tend to view Him as a force rather than a Person, and certainly not a member of the Godhead. In an Orthodox book entitled "A Guide to Jewish

---

[64] Isaiah 6:3
[65] Revelation 4:8
[66] Jeremiah 22:29
[67] Acts 10:16

Knowledge,"[68] the Holy Spirit and the Spirit of God do not even get mentioned.

The Jewish world is noted for its adherence to monotheism, yet it was not always so. The 70-year captivity in Babylonia was to punish and teach the people of Judah, curing them of following a multitude of pagan gods, as was so prevalent even in the time of Jeremiah. However, Jewish understanding of the Godhead is not the same as we find in the Hebrew Bible. One of the most important Jewish philosophers and Torah scholars of the Middle Ages was Moses ben Maimon (Maimonides). It is he who produced the "13 Principles of Faith," which largely counter the claims of the New Covenant.[69] The second principle states, "I believe with perfect faith that the Creator, blessed be His name, is a Unity, and that there is no union in any way like Him. He alone is our God, who was, who is, and who is to be."

This seeks to deny the Tri-unity of the Godhead, and the word used by Maimonides for unity *(yachid)* means a singular, indivisible unity. The word is used in the verse "Make mourning *as for* an only son."[70] But the Biblical word consistently used of the Persons of the Godhead is the word echad, which is a composite unity, as when saying "And all the people answered with one voice."[71] The tombstone of Maimonides in Israel has this inscription – "From Moses to Moses, there was none like Moses." Sadly, the Jewish world to this day has listened to the wrong Moses.

---

[68] Jewish Chronicle Publications, 1958
[69] Another name for the New Testament. See Jeremiah 31:31
[70] Jeremiah 6:26, see also Proverbs 4:3, Zechariah 12:10
[71] Exodus 24:3

In Kabbalah[72] – now so popular among Hollywood actors – a strange philosophy developed in Orthodox Judaism of there being 10 emanations (or enumerations) called *sefirot*, through which God manifests His will. Interestingly, over 10 centuries ago, some rabbis questioned whether such speculations were compatible with monotheism. This mystical teaching has no connection with the apostle John's writing where he mentions "the seven Spirits of God,"[73] which emphasises the seven perfect qualities of the Holy Spirit, one of the only three members of the Godhead.

---

[72] A form of Jewish mysticism
[73] Revelation 5:6

English	Transliteration	Hebrew
The Holy Spirit	Ruakh Ha-Ko-desh	רוּחַ הַקֹּדֶשׁ
The Temple	Beit Ha-Mik-dash	בֵּית הַמִּקְדָּשׁ
sanctified, hallowed	yit-ka-dash	יִתְקַדַּשׁ
Holy, Holy, Holy [is] the Lord of Hosts Isaiah 6:3	Ka-dosh Ka-dosh Ka-dosh Y'hovah Ts-va-ot	קָדוֹשׁ קָדוֹשׁ קָדוֹשׁ יְהֹוָה צְבָאוֹת
wrote (masc sing)	ca-tav	כָּתַב
letter (postal)	mikh-tav	מִכְתָּב
address	c'tov-et	כְּתֹבֶת
The Lord [who] heals	Yehovah Ra-fa	יְהֹוָה רָפָא
doctor	ro-fe	רוֹפֵא
dentist (doctor of teeth)	ro-fe shin-ayim	רוֹפֵא שִׁנַּיִם
healing, or medicine	r'fooah	רְפוּאָה
complete healing	r'fooah sh'lem-ah	רְפוּאָה שְׁלֵמָה
medication, remedy	t'roo-fah	תְּרוּפָה
take not your Holy Spirit from me	Rooakh kd'sh'kha al-ti-kakh mi-men-ni	רוּחַ קָדְשְׁךָ אַל־תִּקַּח מִמֶּנִּי

and grieved His Holy Spirit	v'its-tsvoo et rooakh kad-sho	וְעִצְּבוּ אֶת־רוּחַ קָדְשׁוֹ
The Spirit of the Lord Yehovah is upon Me	Roo-akh Adonai Ye-ho-vah A-lie	רוּחַ אֲדֹנָי יְהוִה עָלָי
Song of Songs	Sheer Ha-Sheer-eem	שִׁיר הַשִּׁירִים
Holy of Holies (most Holy Place)	Kodesh Ha-Kadash-eem	קֹדֶשׁ הַקֳּדָשִׁים
King of kings	Melech Ha-m'la-khim	מֶלֶךְ הַמְּלָכִים
Artaxerxes	Ar-takh-shas-te	אַרְתַּחְשַׁשְׂתְּא
Nebuchadnezzar	N'voo-khad-nets-ar	נְבוּכַדְנֶאצַּר
land or earth (repeated)	Erets, erets, arets	אֶרֶץ אֶרֶץ אֶרֶץ
seraphs	s'rafeem	שְׂרָפִים
cherubs	c'roovim	כְּרֻבִים
only, single	yachid	יָחִיד
one (composite)	ekhad	אֶחָד
Moses	Mo-sheh	מֹשֶׁה

Lesson 8: The Cross

The Hebrew word for the cross is *tslav*. You can see from the chart how the word for Crusaders is derived from that same word. This is, sadly, how many Jewish people see the cross, an object labelling or characterising their murderers and persecutors. As a reading point of revision here the reader can see how the "v" letter contained in the Hebrew word for cross has gained a dagesh and now makes a "b" sound. Paul writes in Galatians 3:13, "Christ has redeemed us from the curse of the law, having become a curse for us (for it is written, "Cursed *is* everyone who hangs on a tree.")"

It is thought that Jesus would have been crucified on rough wood from an olive tree and, in that sense, He hung on a tree and was cursed in His vicarious role. We will take some words from this Old Testament reference for our reading chart.[74] I have also added the phrases for the two trees in the Garden of Eden, the Tree of Life and the Tree of the Knowledge of Good and Evil.

The cross is regarded as offensive for the above reasons in the Jewish world. What we know as the "Red Cross" charity is in Israel the "Red Shield of David," (*Ma-gen Da-vid A-dom*) and you may notice their vehicles and uniforms are marked in this way on news reports following a terrorist outrage in Israel.

Jesus spent the night immediately preceding His arrest praying in a garden named Gethsemane.[75] Opinions differ as to whether this is a Hebrew or an Aramaic name. *Gat* means a "press" and *sh'manay* refers most likely to the oil contained

---

[74] Deuteronomy 21:23
[75] Matthew 26:36

within olives. Therefore, this is a name indicating an olive-press to produce the oil used in those days for lighting, cooking, and religious purposes. What an appropriate name for the place for where Jesus would pour out His soul in prayer until He shed drops of blood. "And being in agony, He prayed more earnestly. Then His sweat became like great drops of blood falling down to the ground."[76]

Pontius Pilate offered to release either Barabbas or Jesus because this was his custom at Passover.[77] Barabbas, as we saw in an earlier lesson, contains the Aramaic for "son of," that is *Bar*, and the word for father. This suggests that it is a title rather than a name. It is possible that this man, Bar Abba, was an anti-Roman gang leader, following his own father in philosophy and action. In a similar way, we may describe a person as "a chip off of the old block!"

Luke tells us that the accusation sign for Jesus on His cross was written in three languages: Greek, Latin and Hebrew. All three languages proclaim that here was the "King of the Jews." I have put that phrase in the chart. We will go through the two words, one at a time, and consider what they teach us about Hebrew grammar.

It is easy enough to read the word for king in the chart, and to make out the three root letters. We follow those root letters in the similar words there. Next we see the Hebrew for "queen" and this shows us how a word (here "king") is typically made feminine by adding a *hey* at the end. The vowels change too. Since the word for king gains a *dagesh* in the word for queen, then the rough *khaf* sound becomes a k sound. We

[76] Luke 22:44
[77] Matthew 27: 15-26

go on to see the Hebrew word for kingdom, and this time the root letters have a *vav* and *tav* added.

We come on to the associated words for kingdom, the Kingdom of Heaven, and the name of the servant of the High Priest whom we encounter at the arrest of Jesus, "Then Simon Peter, having a sword, drew it and struck the high priest's servant, and cut off his right ear. The servant's name was Malchus."[78] Edersheim comments that this is a Greek form of the Hebrew name *Malluch*,[79] which means counsellor.[80] Others say that this name means "king."

While we are on the subject of royalty, the word for "prince" is *Sar*, hence Jesus is *Sar Shalom*, the prince of peace.[81] I have included the related word for princess, which was the name of Abraham's wife, Sarah.

There is another example of related words in the chart showing typical simple grammatical rules, where I give you Hebrew words for boy, boys (or children), girl, childhood, and birthday. You will be able to follow through the root letters and typical ways of forming masculine and feminine plurals.

Among Jesus' last words from the Cross was an Aramaic translation of Psalm 22:1, "My God, My God, why have You forsaken Me?" You can see from the two versions in the chart that the verb, "forsaken," is totally different in Aramaic to the original Hebrew text of the Psalm.[82]

---

[78] John 18:10
[79] 1 Chronicles 6:44, Nehemiah 10:4
[80] The Life and Times of Jesus the Messiah book 5, chapter 12
[81] Isaiah 9:6
[82] Luke 23:46 and John 19:30 provide His very last words.

Robert's comments

The Greek word (stauros) for cross can describe the horizontal piece (Latin – patibulum) or the entire cross, with the patibulum and victim affixed to the vertical section already standing in the ground. The Romans adapted the use of crucifixion from the practice of the Phoenicians, and added a rough seat (sedile), both to add to any victim's suffering and to ensure that the body was secure on the cross. It is most likely that Jesus was crucified on a "Latin cross" – one that had the horizontal bar spaced away from the top of the vertical bar, leaving room for affixing the accusation board. Uniquely, Jesus did not have an accusation stated against Him, but the declaration of Pontius Pilate, the prefect of Judea, that here was the King of the Jews. In his argument with the determined religious leadership of Jerusalem, Pilate would have the last word. The Romans used up so much olive wood for crucifixion in their wars with the Jews in Judea, that eventually there was a great shortage of olive trees in the Land.

In the Crusades of the 11th century onwards, for over two centuries, Jewish communities in Europe, especially Germany, were attacked and many killed. The Crusaders, on their way to take Jerusalem from the Islamic infidels, thought it was a righteous act to kill Jews as "Christ killers." They had crosses forming the artwork on their uniforms and shields. Jewish people are nervous at the sight of crosses, seeing these as symbols of persecution – a far cry from the truth, as Jesus died on the cross out of the deepest love for all men.

Deuteronomy 21:22-23 states that a man put to death because of a crime committed and then hung on a tree was cursed by God. Interestingly, the body was not to remain on the tree overnight. Sin came into the world with Eve, then Adam, eating of forbidden fruit from the Tree of Knowledge of Good and Evil. Jesus, for a short while (six hours), was cursed, not because of any sin of His (there was none), but because He was to be our Divine substitute. He was buried before sunset, and so not left on the tree overnight. In the future, when the earth will no longer be under a curse, we will eat from the Tree of Life.[83]

---

[83] Revelation 22:14

English	Transliteration	Hebrew
cross	ts'lav	צְלָב
Crusader	Tsal-ban	צַלְבָּן
tree	ets	עֵץ
because [of the] curse of God	kee-kil-lat Elohim	כִּי־קִלְלַת אֱלֹהִים
The Tree of Life	Ets Ha-khay-yim	עֵץ הַחַיִּים
Tree of the Knowledge of Good and Evil	Ets Ha-d-da-at Tov va-Ra	עֵץ הַדַּעַת טוֹב וָרָע
Red Shield of David	Magen Da-vid Adom	מָגֵן דָּוִד אָדוֹם
Gethsemane	Gat-Sh'manay	גַּת־שְׁמָנֵי
Barabbas	Bar-abba	בַּר־אַבָּא
King of the Jews	Mel-ekh Ha-Y-hood-eem	מֶלֶךְ הַיְּהוּדִים
king	mel-ekh	מֶלֶךְ
queen	mal-kah	מַלְכָּה
kingdom	mal-khoot	מַלְכוּת
Kingdom of Heaven	Mal-khoot Ha-Sha-mayim	מַלְכוּת הַשָּׁמַיִם

Malchus (Greek)	Mal-khos	מַלְכּוֹס
Malchus (Hebrew)	Mal-lookh	מַלּוּךְ
Prince of Peace	Sar Shalom	שַׂר־שָׁלוֹם
princess	sa-rah	שָׂרָה
boy (or child)	yel-ed	יֶלֶד
boys or children	y'lad-eem	יְלָדִים
girl	yal-dah	יַלְדָּה
childhood	yal-doot	יַלְדוּת
birthday (day of birth)	yom hool-ledet	יוֹם הֻלֶּדֶת
why [have you] forsaken me (Aramaic)	la-mah sh'vak-tanie	לְמָה שְׁבַקְתַּנִי
why [have you] forsaken me (Hebrew)	la-mah azav-tanie	לְמָה עֲזַבְתָּנִי

Lesson 9: Names in the New Testament

Many of us are confused when we turn from the Old to the New Testament and discover that many of the names appear unfamiliar, which in turn adds to the impression of lack of continuity between the two eras.

If we start with the family of the Lord Jesus, His mother's name is recorded in the New Testament as Mary, which seems completely remote from the Old Testament. Actually, her name was Miriam, which is written in this lesson's chart. The name of Jesus' foster father, Joseph, is of course familiar to Old Testament readers. I have put its Hebrew spelling and reading in the chart. James, the half-brother of Jesus, wrote the epistle bearing his name. This is a Greek rendition of Jacob, which is also the name of Joseph's father as recorded in the genealogy of Jesus in the Gospel of Matthew. Thus, we know that this half-brother of Jesus was given the same name as his grandfather. Jude 1:1 is thought to indicate that the author was the half-brother of Jesus and full brother of James. Jude seems a strange name to Old Testament readers. We know the names of two more brothers from Matthew 13:55, "Is this not the carpenter's son? Is not His mother called Mary? And His brothers James, Joses, Simon, and Judas?" Here, Jude is rendered Judas. Both names refer to the Hebrew name Yehuda, which is included in this lesson's chart. Also included is the Hebrew for Judas Iscariot. He is literally Yehuda, a man (*eesh*) from the town of *Kiriot* in the region of Judea.[84]

Most translations render "Joses" as Joseph, the name of the father of Jesus' brothers. "Simon" is "Shimon." This name

---

[84] Joshua 15:25

is translated as "Simeon" in the passage about Jesus being taken as a baby into the Temple courts in Jerusalem.[85]

In the New Testament several women have the name Miriam. We read of "Mary called Magdalene" in Luke 8:2. She was given the name Mary the Magdalete because she was from the village of Magdala on the shores of the Sea of Galilee, about six miles or so south of Capernaum. Then we have Mary, the sister of Lazarus and Martha, from Bethany.

The name of Mary's brother in Hebrew is Eleazer, meaning "God has helped." As you look at this name in Hebrew characters in the chart, you can easily spot the first two letters, *aleph* and *lamed,* as being a Hebrew word for God or god. The name has a similar meaning as the Old Testament name *Azariah* –Yehovah has helped. We notice from the chart the three root letters meaning "helped" in both names in Hebrew.

There is a difference of opinion as to whether Martha (*Marta*) is a Hebrew or Aramaic name, and it is shown in the chart in Hebrew characters. The family of Miriam, Eleazer and Marta lived in a village called Bethany. We already know that *bayit* means a house. Here it sounds a little different, *beit*, since it is in a grammatical construction meaning "house of." Different interpretations are offered for the second word in the phrase, *Anya*. It is often said that it refers to the poor. Thus the name of this village where Jesus loved to visit His friends means "House of the Poor."[86] This is interesting as Jesus read in the synagogue at Nazareth from the scroll of Isaiah, "The Spirit of the LORD *is* upon Me, because He has anointed Me

---

[85] Luke 2:34
[86] Other suggestions are "House of Figs" or "House of Affliction."

to preach the gospel to *the* poor."[87] What a touching thought that those whom the world looked down on because of poverty were the very ones to listen to Him. We may ponder upon the reason why Bethany was the place from which the Lord chose to ascend into heaven.[88]

In addition, remember how we learned that there are two silent letters which can be utilised at the beginning of a word starting with a vowel sound. These are the *aleph* and the *ayin*. One of the Hebrew words for "I" is *ani*, spelt with an *aleph*, and the word for "poor" is *ani* spelt with an *ayin*. David writes in Psalm 40:17, "I *am* poor and needy..." See if you can read this in the Hebrew and recognise the thinly concealed poetry in the first two words. If you are puzzled, the *vav* preceding the first and third words simply means "and."

וַאֲנִי עָנִי וְאֶבְיוֹן

The Hebrew grammar rules can be very technical, and I will explain the use of this *vav* prefix. If you are not particularly interested in fine grammatical details, please disregard the rest of this paragraph. Usually the *vav* prefix has the vowel sound *shv'h* immediately below it, so it sounds like a short "v" sound. However, if the adjacent first letter of the word to which it is attached is what is known as a "labial consonant" then the *vav* gains a dot in the middle and sounds like "oo" instead of "v." The labial consonants are *beit*, *vav*, *mem* and *peh*. The *beit* and *peh* will lose their *dagesh* and will themselves now be

---

pronounced as *veit* and *fey*. There are other complex rules about when the "v" sound becomes "oo."[89]

We continue this section on the names in the family of Jesus by considering Elizabeth (the relative of His mother), Zechariah and their precious son, John. The name Elizabeth means, "my God is an oath." You can see the first two letters of the name in Hebrew form the word for God, *el*, and this is followed by a *yod* which indicates possession, hence "my God." *Sheva* means an oath. It is the same word that crops up in the place name, Beersheba, which means "well of the oath." Elizabeth's priestly husband, Zechariah, has the same name as the Hebrew prophet. The name of God appears in this name too, but at the end: the *yod* and *hey* spell *Yah* and the meaning is "Yah remembers." Their son of promise, John, is *Yokhanan* in Hebrew and means "God is gracious." The first part of the name refers to Yehovah, and the second part to the verb *khanan* meaning to be gracious. I have put the word for grace or favour in the chart. According to Strong's Concordance, this word occurs 69 times in the Old Testament, including the well-known verse about the woman of valour from Proverbs 31:30, where it is translated as charm, grace, or favour: "Charm *is* deceitful and beauty *is* passing, But a woman *who* fears the LORD, she shall be praised." This same word *khen* is at the root of the Old Testament name Hannah which means favour or grace. We see this name in the New Testament as Anna. Do not get this confused with the name, Susannah, which means "lily."

---

[89] See, for example, the website article "The Conjunctive Vav" on the website of Hebrew for Christians.

You will see Joanna[90] also on the chart, which means "God is gracious" or "grace of God." It is clear from the chart that Joanna is the feminine form of John. While we are on the subject of women's names, we read of Salome in Mark's Gospel[91] which is *Shlomit* in Hebrew, and which means peaceful and is from the word *shalom*. It is the feminine form of the Old Testament name, Solomon.

We can move on to examine the names of some of Jesus' apostles. "He chose twelve whom He also named apostles: Simon, whom He also named Peter, and Andrew his brother; James and John; Philip and Bartholomew; Matthew and Thomas; James the *son* of Alphaeus, and Simon called the Zealot; Judas *the son* of James, and Judas Iscariot, who also became a traitor."[92] Using the information we gleaned in a previous lesson, we can see that two of the disciples, named here as James, were Jacob and two rendered as Judas were called *Yehuda*.

John 1:42: "Now when Jesus looked at him, He said, "You are Simon the son of Jonah. You shall be called Cephas" (which is translated, A Stone)." Cephas or *Keefa* (in the chart in Hebrew characters) is an Aramaic word. Peter is a Greek name meaning stone. His other name was Shimon, Bar Jonah. We are now able to recognise this as partly Hebrew and partly Aramaic, Simon, son of Jonah.[93] Jonah, or *Yonah* in Hebrew, means dove. This title is reproduced in the chart for you to read. His is the same name as the one translated Simeon in the previous lesson. Bartholomew means son of *Talmai*. It is

---

[90] Luke 8:3
[91] Mark 15:40
[92] Luke 6:13-16
[93] John 21:15

thought he may well be the same person as Nathaniel. When you read Nathaniel in the chart, you will be able to recognise the final two letters as being *el* (God). The first three letters are from the verb "to give." It means God has given. This is similar to the name Matthew which is gift of Jehovah. This name indicates again the use of a *mem* added to the root letters to form a noun (as mentioned earlier in the lesson on the Holy Spirit). In the chart you will see the root letters for the verb to give, expressed as the masculine singular past tense. Then I show you the noun emanating from the root letters, with the *mem* added, meaning gift. This word is related to the *Matit-ya-hoo.*

The theme of names meaning "God has given" or "gift of God" is a strong one running through the Bible. For this reason, I have included in the chart for this lesson the names Jonathan and Elnathan. They both can be translated "God (either *Yehovah* or *El)* gave" or "gift of God." Incidentally, if you look back in this lesson to the meaning of the name John, you will see that it has an entirely different meaning to Jonathan.

We can end this lesson by noting names which are conspicuous by their absence in the New Testament documents outside the genealogies. For example, men's names like Adam, Isaac, Aaron, David, Michael, Daniel, and Jeremiah and women's names such as Eve, Deborah, and Abigail.

Robert's comments

It is a curious thing to observe how the Jewish world, and that of Christians, view the person of Jacob so differently. How widespread is the conclusion of preachers and Christian laity alike, that Jacob is an unstable character, and something of a sly cheat. Among Jewish people, Jacob is seen as an honourable person, and in this matter, I believe that the Jewish view is the correct one.

Rebekah was told by the LORD when she was pregnant and in great discomfort that two nations were in her womb, and that the elder would serve the younger.[94] God would cut across the usual tradition that the first-born son would be privileged over others. Isaac should have accepted God's will in this matter, but when he was old, he intended blessing Esau. Rebekah's plan to trick Isaac into thinking that Jacob was Esau corrected Isaac's wrong intention.

Additionally, in the comparison of Esau (the skilful hunter) with Jacob, most Bibles say that the latter was "a mild man."[95] In fact, the Hebrew word used is the same as that used to describe Job – perfect or blameless.[96] Is it not better for us to think of Jacob as one who always sought God's blessing, in contrast with profane Esau, who sought to satisfy his stomach? The LORD made a promise to Jacob of territory and of comfort in the dream of a stairway reaching heaven.[97] When he fought God in the night and lived, he was blessed and given the name Israel (fighter with God). 1,600 years after this time, the LORD stated, "Yet Jacob I have loved; but Esau I have hated."[98] Psalms 14 and 53, nearly identical, close by looking forward to the restoration of Israel, as "Let Jacob rejoice *and*

---

[94] Genesis 25:23
[95] Genesis 25:27
[96] Job 1:1
[97] Genesis 28:12-22
[98] Malachi 1:2,3

Israel be glad."[99] The two names here are used interchangeably.

The New Covenant confirms Jacob's name to be valued in the Jewish world. Matthew 1:16 provides the genealogy of Jesus the Messiah, "And Jacob begot Joseph the husband of Mary, of whom was born Jesus who is called Christ." So the father of Joseph, foster-father of Jesus, was Jacob, and in the Jewish world, names of villains are not used for the children – but names of Biblical heroes are. Also, the portrait gallery of heroes of faith in Hebrews 11 includes Jacob in verse 21, when he blessed the sons of Joseph on his deathbed.

---

[99] Psalm 14:7

English	Transliteration	Hebrew
Miriam (Mary)	Mir-yam	מִרְיָם
Joseph	Yo-sef	יוֹסֵף
Jacob, James	Ya-akov	יַעֲקֹב
Yehuda	Y'hoo-dah	יְהוּדָה
Judas Iscariot	Y'hoo-dah Eesh K'ree-yot	יְהוּדָה אִישׁ־ קְרִיּוֹת
Simon or Simeon	Shim-on	שִׁמְעוֹן
Mary called Magdalene	Mir-yam ha-nikra-ah Mag-dal-eet	מִרְיָם הַנִּקְרָאָה מַגְדָּלִית
Lazarus or Eleazar	El-azar	אֶלְעָזָר
Azariah (OT name)	Azar-e-yah	עֲזַרְיָה
Martha	Mar-ta	מַרְתָּא
Bethany	Beit An-ya	בֵּית עַנְיָה
Elizabeth	Elee-shev-a	אֱלִישֶׁבַע
Beersheba	B'er Shev-a	בְּאֵר שֶׁבַע
Zechariah	Z'kh-ar-eyah	זְכַרְיָה

John	Yo-kha-nan	יוֹחָנָן
favour or grace	khen	חֵן
Hannah	Khan-nah	חַנָּה
Susanna	Shosh-an-nah	שׁוֹשַׁנָּה
Joanna	Yo-hanah	יוֹחָנָה
Salome	Sh'lom-eet	שְׁלוֹמִית
Solomon	Shlo-moh	שְׁלֹמֹה
Simon Peter	Shi-mon Petros	שִׁמְעוֹן פֶּטְרוֹס
Cephas	Keefa	כֵּיפָא
Son of Jonah	Bar Yonah	בַּר־יוֹנָה
Bartholomew	Bar Tal-mai	בַּר־תַּלְמַי
Nathaniel	N'tan-el	נְתַנְאֵל
Matthew	Mat-tit-yahoo	מַתִּתְיָהוּ
[he] gave	na-tan	נָתַן
gift	mat-tan-ah	מַתָּנָה
Jonathan	Yo-natan	יוֹנָתָן
Elnathan	El-natan	אֶלְנָתָן

Lesson 10: Hebrew & Aramaic words in the New Testament

It is not always easy for scholars to distinguish between Hebrew and Aramaic words used or quoted in the New Testament. The two languages are closely related. The word "Aramaic" derives from "Aram," an ancient name for Syria. Before the time of Jesus, Aramaic was used by the Persian and Babylonian empires. It became the language of commerce until about A.D. 636.[100] Like Hebrew, Aramaic is a Semitic language. Alfred Edersheim writes that the ordinary people of Jesus' time did not know pure Hebrew. Hebrew was the language of the religious world, being used in the synagogue and by students. He explains that an interpreter was used in the synagogue to translate the Hebrew scriptures read into the spoken language of the time.[101] This observation sheds light on the various modern Bible translations of Acts 22:2, when Paul is making his defence in Jerusalem. Depending on your translation, it will read that the crowd became quiet when they heard him speaking to them in "Aramaic," "their own language," "the Hebrew language," "in Hebrew," and "in the Hebrew dialect."

This is illustrated by the verse "it became known to all those dwelling in Jerusalem; so that field is called in their own language, Akeldama, that is, Field of Blood."[102] Here, we can see from looking at the chart that although the word for blood

---

[100] factsanddetails.com "Aramaic, the language of Jesus, and places where it is still spoken."
[101] The Life and Times of Jesus the Messiah, Book 1, Chapter 1 (1:10,11)
[102] Acts 1:18

is very similar in Aramaic and Hebrew, the words for field are different.

In the Gospel of Mark, Jesus raises the daughter of Jairus, declaring the Aramaic phrase: *Talita cumi*.[103] The first word of this expression may bring to mind the white and blue men's Jewish prayer shawl, the *tallit*, which is also a word with an Aramaic root. You can see from the chart how similar the Hebrew spelling is to *Talita*. We see the second word in the Old Testament in Isaiah 60:1, "Arise, shine; for your light has come! And the glory of the LORD is risen upon you." The first couple of words in English may remind readers of an old advert for a breakfast cereal! In addition, there is a lovely Messianic worship song with the same title on YouTube.[104]

We see another Aramaic word when Jesus heals the deaf man, "Then, looking up to heaven, He sighed, and said to him, *Ephphatha*, that is, "be opened." "[105] I have put the word in the chart in Hebrew letters, even though Aramaic has its own lettering derived from the Phoenician alphabet. The word below it in the chart is a Hebrew word, being the verb "to open." This helps the reader observe the close linguistic similarities between Aramaic and Hebrew and explains why it is not always easy for scholars to be sure which of the two languages is being quoted or referred to in the Greek New Testament manuscripts. Another Aramaic word included in the chart is *reka*, which was the equivalent of us saying to someone in anger, "you idiot." It was really saying that someone was an

---

[103] Mark 5:41
[104] Barry & Batya Segal – Kumi Ori
[105] Mark 7:34

empty head. I have listed the Hebrew word for empty, again showing the strong links between the two languages.

The greeting with which Paul signs off his first letter to the Corinthians is interesting: *Maranatha*. It means "Come O Lord," and is an appropriate word for our dark days as we await the Second Coming. This is a Greek word, but with Aramaic roots. I have included it in the chart so you can see how a Hebrew speaker would pronounce it.

Although Aramaic was the language of the general population in the land of Israel during the time of Jesus, Hebrew was very important for the religious world. We see some of the words in the chart.

We are starting off with the word for the Sabbath, *Shabbat*. The Jewish world has always valued the Sabbath, the seventh day.[106] It is held in high esteem and referred to as the Queen or Bride. I have put in the chart the Hebrew for bride and also for bridegroom and for voice. The reason is that I would like to give my readers the pleasure of reading part of Jeremiah 33:11 in Hebrew, for which you should by now have much of the vocabulary.

קוֹל חָתָן וְקוֹל כַּלָּה קוֹל אֹמְרִים הוֹדוּ אֶת־יְהֹוָה
צְבָאוֹת כִּי־טוֹב

Kol khatan (the voice of the bridegroom) **v'kol kal-lah**
(and the voice of the bride) **kol omreem** (voice [which] says)

---

[106] Moses sets out the feasts of the LORD in Leviticus 23. These comprise Passover, Shavuot (Weeks), Tabernacles and others. It is notable that Sabbath comes first and so every week is rounded off with a major festival.

hodoo (give thanks) **et Yehovah Ts'va-ot** (to the Lord of Hosts) **kee tov** (because [He is] good).

Shabbat comes from the Hebrew root word for resting and sitting down. I have put in the chart the word in modern Hebrew for "he sat," in order to see this verb in action. Some sharp linguists among you readers may be considering that the *beit* and *veit* can change from one to another depending on vowels and position in the word. That in turn may lead to questions about whether this verb "to sit" is related to "sitting *shiva*," which is the term for the seven days of mourning during which traditionally close family gather and sit on low stools and mourn the loss of a loved one. The practice is based on the Biblical account of the friends of Job, who sat with him for seven days and nights. The word *shiva* is the masculine Hebrew word for seven, and this, together with its feminine form, is included in the chart. This brings me to mention that the numbers in Hebrew each have a masculine and a feminine form. So, if you are describing seven boys or seven girls, then you would use a different form of the number. When counting in Hebrew, rather than using the number as an adjective, the feminine form of each number is used. To speak Hebrew fluently, it is essential to know if a noun is masculine or feminine in order to make the adjective agree with it. I have put the religious word Cohen (priest) in the chart and also the plural in the phrase "high priests." The noun is masculine, and in the plural you can see both its typical masculine plural ending and the adjective *gadol* (meaning great), changed to agree with it. You may be familiar with the Hebrew worship song, *Ki Gadol Atah*. If not, you will find it on YouTube.

We come on to Jewish festivals mentioned in the New Testament. We will start with a festival which relates to the word for seven. Acts 2:1 tells us, "When the Day of Pentecost had fully come, they were all with one accord in one place." This counting of the days starts at the second night of Passover in modern Judaism. 49 days, or seven lots of seven days, (or seven weeks) are counted, and the 50th day is the day of Pentecost. The name of the festival is the Hebrew word for weeks, *shav-oo-ot*, as shown in the chart. It is a harvest festival celebrating the wheat harvest.

The Lord Jesus is not only our Passover Lamb, but He was crucified at the time of the Passover. The Last Supper, which Jesus ate together with His disciples, was the Passover meal. In Hebrew this is called *Pesach*. The word for a festival is *khag*, and you can read in the chart the Hebrew for the feast of Passover.

The terms describing the Jewish religious groups in the New Testament can be bewildering, and it helps to examine the Hebrew. The chief priests are often presented alongside the elders.[107] The latter is a term we are familiar with in the church. Interestingly, the Hebrew word for elder is almost identical with the word for beard, a feature in the Jewish religious world of a mature man.

The meaning of the word translated "Pharisees" in English is "separated ones." The New Testament has much to teach us about the heart of the typical Pharisee, such as in Luke 18:11,12: "The Pharisee stood and prayed thus with himself, 'God, I thank You that I am not like other men—extortioners, unjust, adulterers, or even as this tax collector. I fast twice a week; I give tithes of all that I possess.'" This presents an unattractive portrayal of religious pride and complacency

---

[107] Matthew 21:23; 26:3, 47; 27:1

epitomised by their name. We then come on to the Hebrew word for Sadducees. One opinion is that their name is related to Zadok, David's priest, as set out in the second book of Samuel,[108] whose sons are prophetically referred to by Ezekiel as being those who can come near to Yehovah.[109] A different view states that the word for Sadducee is derived from the Hebrew word for righteousness. It is a term of respect for one modern Ultra-Orthodox man to greet another using the term, *tsadeek,* or righteous one. The term may well bring to mind the verse in Isaiah 65:5, those "who say, 'keep to yourself, do not come near me, for I am holier than you!' "

The Sanhedrin was the highest court in ancient Israel and its members were comprised of both Sadducees and Pharisees. It is a Greek word meaning assembly. Now when we read about Jesus before the Sanhedrin in passages such as Mark 14:53-65, perhaps we will have a fresh perspective on the scene, knowing that the spotless Lamb of God was being tried by men belonging to groups whose names indicated that they prided themselves on being set apart and special.[110]

In Matthew 23, Jesus rebuked the scribes and the Pharisees. The scribes were another group which formed part of the Sanhedrin. Their role in the Jewish world included making legal rulings based on their interpretation of the Word of God and their own traditions. They drafted legal documents such as marriage and divorce contracts. They also preserved the Old Testament Scriptures by very carefully copying the text. For this reason, Jesus expected them to know the word of God.

[108] 2 Samuel 15:24-36
[109] Ezekiel 45:15
[110] There were many different groups within the Pharisees. Nicodemus is presented to us in John chapter 3 as being a ruler and by implication member of the Sanhedrin.

Their name in Hebrew means "one who counts." I have included the Hebrew word for number in the chart, which makes use of the root letters and an extra *mem*, often added to a root to form a noun. See how the *pey* of *sofrim* has no *dagesh* in that word, and is pronounced as an "f," and how after the *mem* is added, so is the *dagesh*, and the "f" sound becomes a "p." Hence it is *mispah* and not *misfah*. Incidentally, the usual Hebrew term for the book of Numbers is *B'midbah*, meaning "in the wilderness" and is taken from the fifth word of the first verse. If the reader is puzzling as to the reason for the scribes being referred to as those who count, this is because the task of the scribes included the most meticulous counting of the number of words, columns, and lines.

Jesus addressed the scribes and Pharisees in Matthew 23: 6-10. He explains that they love the best seats and places at feasts and in the synagogues, and pointed out that they love "to be called by men, 'Rabbi, Rabbi.' " He instructed them, "But you, do not be called 'Rabbi'; for One is your Teacher, the Christ, and you are all brethren. Do not call anyone on earth your father; for One is your Father, He who is in heaven." Significantly, Jesus permitted Himself to be addressed as Rabbi by Judas Iscariot.[111] This matter of how to address a religious leader is a little easier to understand when one considers the function of the religious world in society, and the consequential great honour bestowed particularly on the scribes. "Then He said to them in His teaching, "beware of the scribes, who desire to go around in long robes, *love* greetings in the marketplaces..."[112]

---

[111] Matthew 26:25
[112] Mark 12:38

Edersheim casts a helpful light on the reason that Jesus objected to these religious men being addressed as *Rabbi*. He explains that the term means, "my great one."[113] We see in John 20:16 that when Jesus appears to Mary Magdalene after His resurrection from the dead, she addressed Him as *Rabboni*. Some Bible verses refer to this word as an Aramaic greeting and others as Hebrew. The Bible versions generally agree that it means "teacher." Edersheim comments that Mary's greeting may have been a Galilean variant.[114]

We will mention roles in the early church. The Hebrew for Apostle is *shaleeakh* and you can see this further example of a *furtive patach*. The word means an emissary or a sent one. The disciples are *talmidim*, students or followers.

When we read Revelation chapter 19, the Hebrew word *Hallelujah* is proclaimed four times. This means "praise YAH," which is short for Yehovah. You may recognise the part of the word meaning praise, *hallel*. It is also a term for Psalms 113-118, which were chanted in the Temple when the Passover lambs were being slain. How touching that, as the Lamb of God prepared to be the sacrifice for our sins, the hymn which Jesus and His disciples sang at the conclusion of the Passover meal was very likely to have been from the Hallel Psalms.

Hosannah is not the same sort of word; instead, it is an urgent plea for salvation. It means, "please save us." I have put the Old Testament equivalent phrase in the chart from Psalm 118:25. The little word, *na* can be translated as "now" or "please" depending on the context.

---

[113] Life and Times of Jesus the Messiah chapter 8.
[114] The Life and Times of Jesus the Messiah Book 5

Robert's comments

The tallit is currently a garment worn by Orthodox Jews in particular, and draped (rather like a loose scarf) over the man's clothing for morning prayers and during Yom Kippur for all prayers. It is therefore now a prayer shawl, usually made of wool or cotton, or silk, with fringes at the four corners, which should be an aide to remembering the supposed 613 commandments of the Hebrew Bible. The tallit includes blue banding (perhaps a reminder of a heavenly calling for the people of Israel), but the formula for preparing the precise shade of blue has long been lost. Often, it will have black banding instead, as a reminder that the Herodian Temple was destroyed in the year 70. Orthodox Jews additionally wear a fringed prayer vest under their shirts called a *tallit katan*.[115] This is put on each morning with a special prayer of blessing.

Originally, Hebrew men would have worn a very long, comfortable loose-fitting outer garment (just right for the hot desert climate), which would have had the fringes incorporated into its making. A woman who had a very upsetting health condition heard about Jesus, and touched His garment from behind.[116] He would have worn the standard outer garment. During His crucifixion, the Roman soldiers assigned to watch over Jesus took His garments.[117]

Because of persecution in Europe, with Jewish men being conspicuous when wearing the fringed long outer garment, the decision was made in about 1,000 AD, to wear the tallit instead as a prayer shawl.

---

[115] Literally a "small tallit"
[116] Mark 5:27
[117] John 19:23,24

The Pharisees, with their great burden of additional stories and mythological embellishments, are the fathers of Orthodox Judaism. They were religious to the extreme, and although the wealth of moral and other details already existed in New Covenant times[118], it was only in about 250 AD that Rabbi Judah the Prince collated the stories and commentaries which would eventually form the Talmud. When, during the Roman-Judean war of AD 66 – 73, the Herodian Temple was destroyed, the work and influence of the aristocratic Sadducees was finished.

Moses set out a very important principle in Deuteronomy 4:2, that Israel was forbidden to add to the word he commanded, or take away from it – in order to keep the LORD's commandments. Sadducees denied angels existed, and the resurrection from the dead; they took away from the word of God. Today's Liberal and Reform Jews follow them. But the Pharisees heavily added to God's requirements, and Jesus judged this as adding to men's burdens. When the Temple fell, the Pharisees managed to establish a rabbinical college (Yavneh), and created a new Judaism – without Temple and sacrifice, but based on synagogues and substitutes for sacrifice such as, eventually, the study of Talmud. As the Talmud is highly valued, even though it never says, "Thus says the Lord," and includes much occult and hatred of Jesus, it has moulded Orthodox Judaism into something far removed from what Moses stood for.

---

[118] New Testament times

English	Transliteration	Hebrew
field of blood (in Aramaic)	khakal d'ma	חֲקַל דְּמָא
the field of blood (in Hebrew)	s'deh ha-dam	שְׂדֵה הַדָּם
little girl arise	tal-y'ta koomi	טַלְיְתָא קוּמִי
Jewish men's prayer shawl	tal-leet	טַלִּית
fringed prayer tunic (small tallit)	tal-leet ka-tan	טַלִּית קָטָן
arise and shine	koo-mi or-ee	קוּמִי אוֹרִי
be opened (Aramaic)	ip-pat-takh	אֶפְּתַח
opened (modern Hebrew)	pa-takh	פָּתַח
fool	re-ka	רֵקָא
empty	reyk	רֵיק
Maranatha	Maran Ata	מָרַן אֲתָא
Sabbath	Shab-bat	שַׁבָּת
bride	kal-lah	כַּלָּה
bridegroom	kha-tan	חָתָן
voice	kol	קוֹל
[he] sat	ya-shav	יָשַׁב
shiva/seven (m)	shiv-ah	שִׁבְעָה

seven (f)	sheva	שֶׁבַע
priest	Co-hen	כֹּהֵן
The Chief Priests	Ra-oshay HaCo-han-eem	רָאשֵׁי הַכֹּהֲנִים
High Priest	Co-hen Ha-Gad-ol	כֹּהֵן הַגָּדוֹל
High Priests	Co-han-eem G'dol-eem	כֹּהֲנִים גְּדוֹלִים
because You are great	kee gadol Atah	כִּי גָּדוֹל אַתָּה
week	sha-voo-ah	שָׁבוּעַ
oath	sh'vooah	שְׁבוּעָה
Festival of Weeks	Khag Ha-Shavoo-ot	חַג הַשָּׁבוּעוֹת
Festival of Passover	Khag Pesach	חַג פֶּסַח
Feast of Dedication	Kha-nook-kah	חֲנֻכָּה
elder, old person	za-ken	זָקֵן
elders	z'ken-eem	זְקֵנִים
beard	za-kan	זָקָן
Pharisees	Proo-sheem	פְּרוּשִׁים
Sadducees	Ts'd-dook-eem	צְדוּקִים

Zadok	Tsa-dok	צָדוֹק
righteous one	tsa-deek	צַדִּיק
Zadok the Priest	Tsadok Ha- Co-hen	צָדוֹק הַכֹּהֵן
Sanhedrin	San-hed-reen	סַנְהֶדְרִין
scribes	sof-reem	סוֹפְרִים
number	mis-pah	מִסְפָּר
in the wilderness	b' mid-bar	בְּמִדְבַּר
Rabbi	Rab-bee	רַבִּי
Apostle	Sha-lee-akh	שָׁלִיחַ
disciples	tal-meed-eem	תַּלְמִידִים
Hallelujah	Ha-la-loo-yah	הַלְלוּיָה
Hallel	Hal-lel	הַלֵּל
Hosannah	Ho-sha-na	הוֹשַׁע־נָא
save now (Psalm 118:25)	Hosh-eah na	הוֹשִׁיעָה נָא
Hades	She'ol	שְׁאוֹל

Lesson 11: Place names in the New Testament

The first word in this lesson's chart is Israel. You can see the letters for God (*El*) at the end of the word. Israel means "struggles with God," and it was after fighting throughout the night with God that Jacob was given the name Israel.[119]

We continue our lesson on place names with the city of Jerusalem. We are enjoined to "Pray for the peace of Jerusalem."[120] The Hebrew for this is in the chart for you to appreciate the poetry of the words, as the *shin* and *lamed* sounds are repeated in three different ways. You can see from this lesson's reading chart that Jerusalem clearly contains the word for peace, *shalom*. This leaves the first three letters for us to consider. The general view is that these indicate the term for a city, so the meaning is "city of peace." I have come across other views, including that these letters relate to the phrase, "they will see." Isaiah explains to us how God wants us to consider the city: "rejoice with Jerusalem...I will extend peace to her like a river."[121] I have included in the reading chart some Hebrew words relevant to Melchizedek, the king of Salem (peace); Salem is thought to be an early reference to Jerusalem.

Jesus was born in Bethlehem, "House of Bread." A suitable birthplace for the One who said, "I am the bread of life. He who comes to Me shall never hunger, and he who believes in Me shall never thirst." Bethlehem was also the area where lambs destined for Temple sacrifices were reared; again, this is a most apt location for His birth.

---

[119] Genesis 32:22-32
[120] Psalm 122:6
[121] Isaiah 66:10,12

Nazareth was the place where Jesus spent much of his pre-ministry life. "And he came and dwelt in a city called Nazareth, that it might be fulfilled which was spoken by the prophets, 'He shall be called a Nazarene.' "[122] The name of the settlement is probably related to the word for one who watches. Jesus certainly did a lot of watching in his youth in Nazareth and of course calls us to watch and pray. The modern Hebrew word for Christian is *Notsree*. It may seem surprising that these Hebrew words, sound so similar to "Nazirite." You can see from the Hebrew chart that the former is spelled with a *tsade* sound "ts" and the latter with a *zayin*. It is thus a completely different word. The root letters for Nazirite indicate that it means one who is set apart or consecrated. The distinction can be illustrated in the life of the Apostle Paul. "He had *his* hair cut off at Cenchrea, for he had taken a vow."[123] This was probably a Nazirite vow. Later, in the book of Acts, he was accused before the high priest Ananias of being "a ringleader of the sect of the Nazarenes."[124] This is clearly a reference to being a leader in the early Church.

Israel, at the time of Jesus, was divided into five political divisions. The New Testament concentrates on three of them: Galilee, Judea, and Samaria.[125] We get a snapshot of this in John's Gospel, "He left Judea and departed again to Galilee. But He needed to go through Samaria."[126] Although He was born in Bethlehem, in Judea, and was taken to Egypt as a young child to save His life, Yeshua spent His formative years

[122] Matthew 2:23
[123] Acts 18:18
[124] Acts 24:5
[125] The other two areas were Perea and Decapolis, both beyond the River Jordan. (Blueletterbible.org, article by Don Stewart).
[126] John 4:3,4

living in Galilee. He grew up and resided in Nazareth until, just prior to starting His public ministry, He moved to Capernaum in Galilee. "And leaving Nazareth, He came and dwelt in Capernaum, which is by the sea, in the regions of Zebulun and Naphtali."[127] The term Galilee is derived from the word for "to roll" and hence "rolling," and indeed it is an area of rolling hills. The lake in Galilee is referred to in various ways in the Scriptures. In the Old Testament it is called the Sea of Kinnereth.[128] This relates to its harp-like shape, and is the modern Hebrew term for the Sea of Galilee. It is also referred to in the New Testament as the Lake of Gennesaret,[129] which is a Greek form of Kinnereth. There are many associated words in Hebrew using the root letters for Galilee, and I have put the word for "wave" in the chart. We know how the waves roll before they break. I was interested to hear on a visit to Israel, that following the figures released for the latest depth of the Sea of Galilee is a national pastime for Israelis. This is quite understandable, given that it is Israel's main source of fresh water. In addition, Israel is obliged to obtain a sizeable proportion of its water from the Mediterranean Sea via desalination plants. I have put into the chart the name used in Israel for the Mediterranean Sea. This Hebrew term is translated, "The Middle Sea."[130]

The other big area of water in Israel is the Dead Sea, the lowest point on earth, approximately 1,400 feet below sea level. The falling water levels here are also very concerning. It is helpful to look at the spelling of the Dead Sea, called the

---

[127] Matthew 4:13
[128] Numbers 34:11
[129] Luke 5:1
[130] The Old Testament has various names for the Mediterranean Sea, see "Balashon – Hebrew Language Detective" website under *tichon*.

"Salt Sea" in Hebrew.[131] You will notice that the Hebrew for "salt" sounds rather like the word for king. Both words are similar to the Hebrew word for angel, which I have also included in the chart. Just as in English, where two words in Hebrew sound similar, be careful of jumping to the conclusion that they are related.

"Woe to you, Chorazin! Woe to you, Bethsaida! For if the mighty works which were done in you had been done in Tyre and Sidon, they would have repented long ago, sitting in sackcloth and ashes. But it will be more tolerable for Tyre and Sidon at the judgment than for you. And you, Capernaum, who are exalted to heaven, will be brought down to Hades."[132]

Strong's Concordance says that the name Chorazin is of uncertain origin; others suggest that it indicates a mystery or hidden secret. Bethsaida is not to be confused with Bethesda, the pool in Jerusalem, "Now there is in Jerusalem by the Sheep *Gate* a pool, which is called in Hebrew, Bethesda, having five porches."[133] This is yet another example of the relevant Hebrew root letters indicating that two words, apparently similar to our English ears, can be totally different. Interestingly, some of the Bible versions say that Bethesda is in the Hebrew language, and some that it is Aramaic. It is more accurate to say, when we come across such words, "the Hebrew spoken dialect of the day, which was Aramaic." You can see how very different the two names, Bethsaida and Bethesda, are in Hebrew by looking at the chart. The former means "house of the

---

[131] The Romans called the Dead Sea, the Asphalt Sea.
[132] Luke 10:13-15 (American spelling retained due to copyright)
[133] John 5:2

fisherman or hunter," and the latter is "the house of *khesed*," meaning merciful kindness.

We come on to the base Jesus used for His public ministry, Capernaum. This means the village of Nahum – apparently not a reference to the Old Testament prophet Nahum. His name means "comforter." So, a secondary meaning is that it is the village of comfort. The name is thought to be related to the name for Noah, which means rest. If you read Noah's name from the chart, you will see a further example of the furtive patach, which means that the vowel sound under the *khet* is read before the last letter. There is a similar sounding woman's name in the Bible, Noah. In fact, if you look up online the second half of Numbers 26:33 in Hebrew, which would be good reading practice, you may recognise some of the words from our studies. The verse says: "and the names of the daughters of Zelophehad *were* Mahlah, Noah, Hoglah, Milcah, and Tirzah." This is yet another example of what appears to be the same word in English being totally different in the original Hebrew. Noah is thought to be related to the root for shaking or staggering, and suggests movement.

It is interesting that Peter was recognised as coming from Galilee because of the way he spoke.[134] Alfred Edersheim explains the reasons why the religious world in Israel looked down on those from Galilee.[135] They were disapproved of for grammatical errors, including mispronunciation.[136] In modern Israel, the main differences in speech relate to whether the speaker is from a Sephardi background (areas such as North Africa) or Ashkenazi (such as Western Europe and the USA).

---

[134] Matthew 26:73
[135] John 4:9
[136]The Life and Times of Jesus the Messiah book 2, chapter 9.

There will also be some influence depending on whether Yiddish is spoken at home. Yiddish was spoken by Ashkenazi Jews in Europe, being a mixture of German and Hebrew with a smattering of other languages. Curiously, it is written with Hebrew letters, with largely German pronunciation! For example, in Yiddish *Shabbat* is pronounced *Shabbos*. It is still spoken by some communities, especially among the ultra-Orthodox.

Samaria, or *Shomron* in Hebrew, means a place to watch, such as a watchtower. I am including in the chart for this lesson the few words for "Yehovah will keep you." This is from Psalm 121:7 and illustrates the verb to keep, in the sense of watching over. We are all familiar with Jesus' encounter with a Samaritan woman in John chapter 4, when He had to go through the region of Samaria. We are told in verse 9 that Jews do not associate with Samaritans. We see from verse 20 that there is a sharp division as to religious practice: "Our fathers worshiped on this mountain, and you *Jews* say that in Jerusalem is the place where one ought to worship." Yet the woman was expecting the Messiah; she "said to Him, "I know that Messiah is coming" (who is called Christ). "When He comes, He will tell us all things." " There are detailed historical reasons for the divisions between Jews and Samaritans, which are explained at the end of this lesson. The parable of the Good Samaritan illustrates the disdain felt by the Jews towards the Samaritans, and the division between the two groups.[137]

The good news of the death and resurrection of the Lord Jesus made inroads into this ancient hostility between Jews and Samaritans. We read of Peter and John in Acts 8:25, "So when they had testified and preached the word of the Lord, they

[137] Luke 10:25-37

returned to Jerusalem, preaching the gospel in many villages of the Samaritans." I have put part of that verse in the chart to illustrate a point of grammar in Hebrew. You learned the word for "village" when we considered Capernaum. As it is a masculine word, it takes the masculine plural ending. The adjective "many" follows the noun, and it too takes the masculine plural ending to agree with the noun. I have put in the chart the word for exalted or many, *rav*, and it is the same word we encountered when we examined the word, "rabbi." We can see that grammar dictates that in the masculine plural, the adjective gains a *dagesh* and the "v" sound becomes a "b." I have also included an example of the feminine adjective, a "big thank you," or "thank you very much." Typically, the feminine has a *hey* suffix to agree with the noun. A related word is the imperative "give thanks" as in Psalm 136 and sung beautifully by Barry and Batya Segal, and obtainable on YouTube.[138]

Judea is largely the land given to the tribe of Judah, the name Latinised by the Romans as Judea. Settlements in Judea whose names we would recognise include Jerusalem, Bethlehem, Bethany, Arimathea, Emmaus, Joppa and Bethphage. Bethphage was the place where Jesus sent two of His disciples to find the donkey and her colt for Him to ride for His entry into Jerusalem. The name means house of young or unripe figs, which is significant as the following day He curses a fig tree for not producing fruit. Figs make an unusual Bible study. Adam and Eve sewed together fig leaves for clothes in Genesis 3:7, and the Lord replaced them with animal skins. Jesus saw Nathanael under the fig tree. Crucially for the age we are living in, the fig tree is also used as a picture of Israel. Jesus instructs us to learn to recognise when His return is drawing near. He

---

[138] Hodu La'Adonai Ki Tov

explains the signs of His coming[139] and uses the fig tree as an illustration:[140] "Now learn this parable from the fig tree: when its branch has already become tender and puts forth leaves, you know that summer *is* near." So, although we have had famines, pestilences, wars, rumours of war and suchlike throughout history, we know that these are signifying the return of Jesus when they occur soon after the rebirth of the Jewish nation, the budding of the fig tree.[141]

We have looked so far in these lessons at the largely self-righteous mindset of the religious world, centred in Jerusalem in Judea. We have considered the area of Galilee where Jesus spent most of His earthly life. We perhaps have more understanding of the geography, tensions and background of Luke 9: 51-53 "Now it came to pass, when the time had come for Him to be received up, that He steadfastly set His face to go to Jerusalem, and sent messengers before His face. And as they went, they entered a village of the Samaritans, to prepare for Him. But they did not receive Him, because His face was *set* for the journey to Jerusalem." We may see the instruction given by Jesus after His resurrection in a slightly different light, "But you shall receive power when the Holy Spirit has come upon you; and you shall be witnesses to Me in Jerusalem, and in all Judea and Samaria, and to the end of the earth." All the disciples were from Galilee, except for Judas Iscariot. We read in Matthew's Gospel that Jesus spoke to the women and said to them, "Do not be afraid. Go *and* tell My brethren to go to Galilee, and there they will see Me... Then the eleven disciples went away into Galilee, to the mountain which Jesus had

---

[139] The Olivet Discourse, Matthew 24 and 25
[140] Matthew 24:32
[141] God's Prophetic Agenda for the End of Days! Johannes Facius

appointed for them."[142] Perhaps since it was their home territory, Jesus did not need to mention Galilee specifically in His commission.

"And when they had come to a place called Golgotha, that is to say, Place of a Skull …"[143] As well as being a place, Golgotha is also the Aramaic word for skull. It is probable that the rock formation at the site resembled a skull with two large sunken eyes. If you have visited Israel, you may have seen this place of the skull near the Garden Tomb (or "Gordon's Tomb"), an area that had been a well-worked limestone quarry. The chart provides the spelling of the word for skull in both Aramaic and Hebrew. You may well spot that the word makes use of the root for "roll" or "wave" and indeed the skull is circular in shape. Now, perhaps by considering the short word, *gal*, we can start to appreciate even more deeply the determined sacrifice of the One who willingly left the rolling hills of beautiful Galilee, travelled through the hostile area of Samaria, and willingly was crucified for our sins at the place of the skull. The term Calvary, so familiar to us in writing, hymns, and sermons, comes from Latin, not from Greek.

We will end this lesson by considering two mountains. They both relate to the End Times. *Har Megiddo* is the Hebrew for Armageddon, the staging post for the great battle for Jerusalem when all nations come against her.[144] As for the Mount of Olives, the disciples were told, "Men of Galilee, why do you stand gazing up into heaven? This *same* Jesus, who was taken up from you into heaven, will so come in like manner as you

---

[142] Matthew 28:10,16
[143] Matthew 27:33
[144] Revelation 16:16. See chapter 11 "Exploring the End Times and Interceding for Israel" for a fuller explanation.

saw Him go into heaven."[145] Just as the risen Lord Jesus ascended into heaven from the Mount of Olives, He will, at His Second Coming, return to the same place. Great things will happen at that time: "And in that day His feet will stand on the Mount of Olives, which faces Jerusalem on the east. And the Mount of Olives shall be split in two, from east to west, *making* a very large valley; half of the mountain shall move toward the north and half of it toward the south."[146]

Robert's comments

Jerusalem – City of Peace, a name yet to be fulfilled! How many cities have had to endure as much invasion, suffering and destruction as she has? Seven times in Deuteronomy, the phrase is used which refers to a settlement where the LORD would establish His name.

Eventually, after David captured the hill of Zion and its environs, Jerusalem would become the national capital 3,000 years ago. 1 Kings 8:16 is one of the Scriptures demonstrating its great importance in God's economy: "Since the day that I brought My people Israel out of Egypt, I have chosen no city from any tribe of Israel *in which* to build a house, that My name might be there; but I chose David to be over My people Israel." So here, the house of glory (Solomon's Temple) would be established, and later the Herodian Temple of New Covenant times would be built on the same site.

The city has been destroyed twice and attacked over 50 times in its history. Taken by General Allenby from the

---

145 Acts 1:11,12
146 Zechariah 14:4

Ottoman Empire in 1917, it was the obvious choice for the re-emerged State of Israel as capital in May 1948. It has an assured future unmatched by that of any other city on earth. Zechariah 14 predicts that, as the nations will be commanded to go up to Jerusalem to worship the King each year at Tabernacles, it will be the national capital and world capital under the LORD's ruling.[147]

Moving on to Bethlehem, the prophet Micah provided a wonderful prediction of the first coming of Jesus the Messiah of Israel. "But you, Bethlehem Ephrathah, *though* you are little among the thousands of Judah, *yet* out of you shall come forth to Me the One to be Ruler in Israel, whose goings forth *are* from of old, from everlasting."[148] The land of Israel had two Bethlehems – that in the territory of Zebulun in Galilee, and Bethlehem Ephrathah, or Bethlehem Judah. Micah pinpoints the small settlement of Judah, hometown of David, as the place where One would come forth to be ruler in Israel (that will be fulfilled at the Second Coming), and who has always been in existence. This can be none other than Jesus the Messiah, the God-Man who graciously appeared to Israel.

Regarding the history of the relationship between the Samaritans and the Jews, we have to go back to the Old Testament books of Kings and Chronicles. Rehoboam succeeded to the throne of his father Solomon. After King Rehoboam's heavy taxation of the people of Israel, the northern 10 tribes rebelled under Jeroboam, and so the united state was divided into two smaller states. The northern territory retained the name Israel, with the capital at Shechem. Golden calves were set up at Dan in the north, and Bethel farther south, with a

---

[147] Zechariah 14:16
[148] Micah 5:2

false priesthood. Judah (with Benjamin) comprised the southern state, retaining Jerusalem as capital with the Temple of Solomon in service. However, Judah would have people from all the tribes of Israel. We learn in Chronicles that the priests (Cohanim) and Levites plus others came to Jerusalem, seeking the LORD God.[149]

Owing to the depth of sin by northern Israel, the Assyrians overwhelmed that land in 722 BC. "So Israel was carried away from their own land to Assyria."[150] The Assyrians then brought people to Israel from Babylon and other areas, to be settled around the environs of Samaria. Intermarrying with the remnants of Israel's population, they worshipped a multitude of gods, compromising the service to the true God. This caused many of the people in Judah to develop a long-lasting hatred of the Samaritans.

---

[149] 2 Chronicles 11:13-17
[150] 2 Kings 17:23

English	Transliteration	Hebrew
Israel	Yis-ra-el	יִשְׂרָאֵל
Jerusalem	Y'roosh-a-lie-im	יְרוּשָׁלַיִם
peace	sha-lom	שָׁלוֹם
pray for the peace of Jerusalem	sh-aloo shalom Y'roosh-a-lie-im	שַׁאֲלוּ שְׁלוֹם יְרוּשָׁלָ͏ם
city	ear	עִיר
they will see	yir-oo	יִרְאוּ
Melchizedek	Mal-kee-tsekek	מַלְכִּי־צֶדֶק
King of Salem	Melekh Sha-lem	מֶלֶךְ שָׁלֵם
Priest of the Most High God	Co-hen l'El El-yon	כֹּהֵן לְאֵל עֶלְיוֹן
Bethlehem	Beit-Le-khem	בֵּית־לֶחֶם
Nazareth	N'tser-et	נְצֶרֶת
Nazarene	Nats-ree	נָצְרִי
Christian	Nots-ree	נוֹצְרִי
Nazirite	N'zeer	נָזִיר
Galilee	Ha-Gal-eel	הַגָּלִיל
Judea or Judah	Y'hood-ah	יְהוּדָה

Samaria	Shom-ron	שׁוֹמְרוֹן
Capernaum	K'far-Na-khoom	כְּפַר־נַחוּם
wave	gal	גַּל
Sea of Galilee (1)	Yam Ha-gal-eel	יַם־הַגָּלִיל
Sea of Galilee (2)	Yam Kin-ne-ret	יָם־כִּנֶּרֶת
harp	ki-noor	כִּנּוֹר
Mediterranean (The Middle Sea)	Ha-Yam Ha-Tee-khon	הַיָּם הַתִּיכוֹן
Dead Sea	Yam Ha-Mel-akh	יָם הַמֶּלַח
angel	mal-akh	מַלְאָךְ
The Angel of the Lord	Mal-akh Yehovah	מַלְאַךְ יְהוָה
The Great Sea	HaYam HaGa-dol	הַיָּם הַגָּדוֹל
Chorazin	Kor-a-zeen	כּוֹרָזִין
Bethsaida	Beyt-Tsy-dah	בֵּית־צָיְדָה
Bethesda	Beyt Khas-da	בֵּית־חַסְדָּא
lovingkindness	khe-sed	חֶסֶד
Noah	Noakh	נֹחַ
Noah (f)	No-ah	נֹעָה
many, great	rav	רַב

in many villages	bi-kh-fareem ra-beem	בִּכְפָרִים רַבִּים
thank you very much	to-dah ra-bah	תּוֹדָה רַבָּה
give thanks to Yehovah because He is good	hodoo la Ye-ho-vah kee tov	הוֹדוּ לַיהֹוָה כִּי־טוֹב
The Lord will watch over you	Yehovah Y'sh-ma-rekha	יְהֹוָה יִשְׁמָרְךָ
Bethphage	Beyt Pa-gay	בֵּית־פַּגֵּי
fig or fig tree	t'enah	תְּאֵנָה
circle	ma-gal	מַעְגָּל
Golgotha, skull (Aramaic)	Gal-gal-ta	גָּלְגָּלְתָּא
skull (Hebrew)	gool-gol-et	גּוּלְגּוֹלֶת
Armageddon	Har M'gid-do	הַר מְגִדּוֹ
Mount of Olives	Har Ha-Zay-teem	הַר הַזֵּיתִים

Lesson 12: Old Testament verses

We will conclude our lessons with a few texts from the Hebrew Bible which are quoted in the New Testament. I will draw these simple verses from two books: firstly, the Gospel of Matthew, since it was written with Jewish readers in mind, and, secondly, the book of Hebrews, as it was specifically addressed to the Hebrew people.

"The LORD said to my Lord." [151]

נְאֻם יְהוָה לַאדֹנִי

This is an extract from the verse Jesus quoted to the Pharisees from Psalm 110:1. We learned earlier that Jewish people will not say the word *Yehovah*; and instead it is read as *Adonai*. There is a problem with that system in this verse. The LORD who is speaking to David's Lord is Yehovah. The Hebrew for the Lord who is being addressed is literally "my Lord" or *Adon-ee*. This is a most important verse, quoted by Mark[152] and also by Peter in his sermon on the Day of Pentecost.[153] A word used as a substitute for God among religious Jews is *Ha Shem*, meaning "the Name." I have seen a Jewish presentation of the reading of this verse in which the rabbi reads, *HaShem* says to *Adonee*.[154]

---

[151] Matthew 22:44, the entire verse reads: "The LORD said to my Lord, "Sit at My right hand, till I make Your enemies Your footstool.""
[152] Mark 12:36
[153] Acts 2:34
[154] Rabbi Toviah Singer, "The Lord said to my Lord?" YouTube

"Blessed *is* He who comes in the name of the LORD!"[155]

בָּרוּךְ הַבָּא בְּשֵׁם יְהוָה

This verse was quoted by Jesus.[156] Here, the word order is the same as in the English. *Barukh* is the word for "blessed" which we encountered when we looked at the Hebrew blessings for bread, wine, and the lighting of candles. There is another word in Scripture also translated "blessed." An example is the verse, "Blessed *is* the man who walks not in the counsel of the ungodly,"[157] which reads as follows in Hebrew:

אַשְׁרֵי הָאִישׁ אֲשֶׁר לֹא הָלַךְ בַּעֲצַת רְשָׁעִים

The above verse from Psalm 1 is another example of the hidden poetry which we do not pick up in our English translations. The first three words are in this lesson's chart. Read them aloud and savour the alliteration and the connection of sounds. The word for "who" or "which" — *asher* — is very similar to the word for blessed, which in turn is linked to the word for happy.

"The stone which the builders rejected has become the chief cornerstone."[158]

אֶבֶן מָאֲסוּ הַבּוֹנִים הָיְתָה לְרֹאשׁ פִּנָּה

---

155 Psalm 118:26
156 Matthew 23:39. The entire verse reads "for I say to you, you shall see Me no more till you say, 'Blessed *is* He who comes in the name of the LORD!'"
157 Psalm 1:1
158 Psalm 118:22. Matthew 21:42

Jesus quoted this verse when He asked the Chief Priests and Elders at the Temple whether they had ever read it in the Scriptures. As you examine the verse in Hebrew, you can see the words for "chief cornerstone," *rosh pinnah. Rosh* means "head" or "first." You will perhaps recognise it from one of the words for the Jewish new year, *Rosh HaShanah*, which literally means, "head of the year." As *shanah* is a feminine word, Jewish people wish one another *Shanah Tovah*, "a good new year." I have given you the term for the Day of Atonement which falls only 10 days after *Rosh HaShanah*. The word for day is *yom*, which is a masculine word with which the adjective must agree. Hence, the greeting *yom tov*, which is also a reference to a festival day.

"You *are* My Son, today I have begotten You."[159]

בְּנִי אַתָּה אֲנִי הַיּוֹם יְלִדְתִּיךָ

We have now moved on to verses quoted in the book of Hebrews. Regarding this verse, we have considered the first word, *ben*, meaning son. The *yod* at the end indicates "my son." We have learned the word *atah* meaning "you."[160] Next, we see *ha* added to *yom* (day), making it mean "today." At the end of the sentence, we can see the root letters from the word for child, *yeled*.[161]

"Your throne, O God, *is* forever and ever."[162]

כִּסְאֲךָ אֱלֹהִים עוֹלָם וָעֶד

The word for throne is the same as for chair, and there is a suffix indicating the pronoun "your." It is a word worth considering because, although it is a masculine word, it has a typically feminine plural ending. I have illustrated this in the chart with the phrase "good chairs." We then come on to the word, *Elohim*, which is a plural word which can either mean God or gods. Genesis 1:1 provides a most interesting verb construction relating to this word for God.

בְּרֵאשִׁית בָּרָא אֱלֹהִים אֵת הַשָּׁמַיִם וְאֵת הָאָרֶץ

In English, it reads "in the beginning God created the heavens and the earth." Almost all the Bible translations agree on this exact wording. The preposition for "in" is the single letter *beit*, and it is added as a prefix to the first word. The word for beginning is related to the word for head, *rosh*. *Elohim*, the third word, is clearly a plural noun (which is the reason it can also mean gods). However, and significantly, the second word, the verb *bara*, is a singular verb. This is a strong hint at the plurality of the Godhead.

"Here am I and the children whom God has given Me."[163]

הִנֵּה אָנֹכִי וְהַיְלָדִים אֲשֶׁר נָתַן־לִי יְהוָה

---

162 Hebrews 1:8 quotes Psalm 45:6
163 Hebrews 2:13 quotes Isaiah 8:18

To help you navigate this verse in Hebrew, the first four words are in the same order as in the English translation. We can recognise the word for children, which we have listed before. Then once more we have the Hebrew for "which"(*asher*). Moving on to the final words of the verse, we read, *natan lee*. Hopefully this will remind you of when we earlier considered the meaning of the names Jonathan and Elnathan.[164] The *lee* indicates the word for "me," and the verse finishes with the word *Yehovah*.

"You *are* a priest forever according to the order of Melchizedek."[165]

אַתָּה-כֹהֵן לְעוֹלָם עַל-דִּבְרָתִי מַלְכִּי-צֶדֶק

We should recognise most of the words in this phrase, including the components of the name Melchizedek, King of Righteousness. We considered the latter part of the name when we examined the origins of the word "Sadducee." The book of Hebrews also describes him as "king of Salem, meaning "king of peace." "[166] I have inserted the last part of that phrase in this lesson's Hebrew chart. The other names are in the chart for our previous lesson.

"The days are coming, declares the Lord, when I will make a new covenant with the people of Israel and with the people of Judah."[167]

---

[164] Lesson 9
[165] Hebrews 5:6 quotes Psalm 110:4
[166] Hebrews 7:2
[167] Hebrews 8:8 quotes Jeremiah 31:31

הִנֵּה יָמִים בָּאִים נְאֻם־יְהוָה וְכָרַתִּי אֶת־בֵּית יִשְׂרָאֵל וְאֶת־בֵּית יְהוּדָה בְּרִית חֲדָשָׁה

We can break down much of this verse using the lessons we have learned in this book. We have considered the word *hinneh* meaning "behold." Then the plural of *yom*, meaning "day," is *ya-meem*. Earlier in this lesson, we looked at the verse in Hebrew, "Blessed is He who comes in the name of the Lord." There the verb "comes" is *ba* (singular). In the verse we are examining in Jeremiah, we have the plural of that verb, so it is *ba-im*. After *ba-im*, we have the Hebrew for "declares Yehovah." *Beit* means "house of." The verse speaks of the "house of Israel" and the "house of Judah." The last two words of the sentence *Brit Khadashah* are also the Hebrew term for the New Testament. We also see the short word *et* twice in this verse; this is something we do not have in English and it points to the direct object of the sentence.[168]

Robert's comments

Psalm 110 begins by stating that it is Davidic, and immediately sets out "The LORD said to my Lord, 'Sit at My right hand, till I make Your enemies Your footstool.'" Jesus sought to show the Pharisees in Matthew 22:41-46 that this psalm prophetically speaks of Himself as Messiah, who will ultimately be honoured. Religious Jews should have been happy to acknowledge

---

[168] See also the interesting internet article on the significance of Jesus being the *aleph* and the *tav* (the first and last letters of the Hebrew alphabet) and Revelation 22:13 (Hebrew4Christians.com : Yeshua and the Hebrew alphabet). When we considered Genesis 1:1 earlier in this lesson, we saw the little word *et* (with a slightly different vowel) pointing to that which God created, namely the heavens and the earth.

the Messiah as Lord. When asked whose Son is He, they correctly replied, "the Son of David," as the Messiah of Israel would have to come from David's line.

We note that Jesus commented, "How then does David in the Spirit call Him 'Lord?'" thus showing that the Holy Spirit moved David to record the words of the psalm. Later, He challenged the Pharisees to think about how the Lord can be David's Son. Of course, we know the answer – that both Miriam (Jesus' mother) and Joseph (His foster father) were of the House of David. We can now interpret Matthew 22:45, seeing it as teaching that Yehovah (the Father) addresses Jesus the Messiah (Lord – also the Son of God) and promises Him the place of highest honour until His enemies are trodden down. After Jesus' terrible suffering on our behalf, His resurrection and ascension to heaven, Jesus was seated at the right hand of God. Additionally, after the Second Coming, Jesus will be honoured by the national conversion of Israel. He will destroy the enemies of God and Israel.

"The stone which the builders rejected has become the chief cornerstone." Mark's Gospel shows us a confrontation between the chief priests, scribes, and elders versus Jesus in Herod's Temple courts.[169] Jesus spoke to them in parables, including the one about the vinedressers killing the heir's son.[170] It contained a warning that the vinedressers (the group confronting Him) would be destroyed, and the vineyard would be given to others. The corrupt Jewish establishment was doomed – and the Lord would be blessing His true followers in their place. Jewish believers in Jesus –"the remnant"– would be blessed alongside those called out from the Gentile world.

---

[169] Mark 12:10-12
[170] Mark 12:2

The religious leaders understood the implication of the parable; Jesus gave a plain warning to this religious group. There is an ancient story that when Solomon's Temple was being built, a stone was cast aside which should have been the cornerstone. Jesus challenged them as to whether they had ever read this Scripture. It clearly relates to Himself – teaching that the One rejected by the builders is central to God's purposes.

English	Transliteration	Hebrew
blessed, happy	ash-rey	אַשְׁרֵי
the man	ha-eesh	הָאִישׁ
who, which	ash-er	אֲשֶׁר
tribal name, meaning "happy"	Ash-er	אָשֵׁר
New Year	Rosh Ha-Shanah	רֹאשׁ הַשָּׁנָה
Happy New Year	Shanah tovah	שָׁנָה טוֹבָה
Yom Kippur	Yom Kip-poor	יוֹם כִּפּוּר
good day	yom tov	יוֹם טוֹב
chair or throne	kis-e	כִּסֵּא
good chairs	kis-ot tov-eem	כִּיסְאוֹת טוֹבִים
God or god	El	אֵל
God or gods	El-o-him	אֱלֹהִים
Behold, here I am!	hin-neh	הִנֵּה
King of Peace	Mel-ekh Ha-Sha-lom	מֶלֶךְ הַשָּׁלוֹם

Moving Forward

I am making suggestions here both for the benefit of those who are potential Hebrew Bible students and for those of you more focused on the creative side.

Readers who want to build up their Hebrew gently, may like to start by searching out further straightforward extracts from Old Testament verses quoted in the New Testament. These will provide material for further consideration. Hebrew New Testaments are available in print and online.

The biggest challenge in getting to grips with a language is the verb structure. This is a huge subject upon which I have deliberately hardly touched. However, I will at this stage mention that in Biblical Hebrew a *vav* is used as a prefix to the verb to indicate the future tense. However, a *vav* can also be used as a prefix to a verb, simply meaning "and," without altering the tense. I will illustrate below with two phrases. The first one is translated "he will speak."[171] The second phrase means "and he spoke of trees."[172]

וְדִבֶּר־הוּא

וַיְדַבֵּר עַל־הָעֵצִים

Many of my readers will be enthusiastic to incorporate simple Hebrew words in their prayer life, worship, song and poetry writing, or in arts and crafts. For these readers, I am including in this section a small sample of simple worship words from the Bible. I will present them both with the

---

[171] Exodus 4:16
[172] 1 Kings 4:33

vowels, for pronunciation purposes, and without, for visual use. Again, further examples can be readily found in a Hebrew Bible. The column without the vowels will familiarise the reader with the appearance of Hebrew text with just the consonants.

Hebrew is a tool to assist us, both in personal meditation upon the Scripture and in ministering to others. I can illustrate this with a personal recent experience. I was very struck, as I wrote this book, by the Aramaic phrase, "Be opened," which we looked at in Lesson 10. We examined the connection with the Hebrew verb "to open." The Aramaic command, in turn, brought to my mind the Scripture in Psalm 81:10, "Open your mouth wide, and I will fill it." I was most interested to see that the Hebrew words used in that verse for opening the mouth is completely different. I have put three words from that verse at the end of this lesson. The first (after the initial *hey*) uses the root letters for growing wide. The second is the word for mouth, which we have already encountered (*peh*), with a suffix indicating possession. So the meaning is, "Let your mouth grow large or wide." This led me to consider the name Rahab,[173] spelt with a *khet*, which means to be spacious, as it also makes use of the root letters for growing wide. I also read in my research that there is another Rahab in the Bible, spelled with a *hey*. This second word with the same spelling in English, has a completely different meaning, relating to being proud or arrogant, and was used to refer to Egypt.[174]

If you have any Jewish friends, it is a powerful witness to them that you are taking the time and trouble to study the

---

[173] Joshua 2:3
[174] Abarim Publications on meaning of Rahab I and Rahab II internet article, accessed 4th July 2022

language of the Old Testament. The Hebrew Bible is known to Jewish people as the *Tanakh*. This term is formed from the initials of each of its three divisions. **T**orah, the Law of Moses (the first five books of the Bible), **N**eviim the prophets, and **K**etuvim, the writings.[175] The Apostle Paul expressed the desire of his heart in the following words, "if by any means I may provoke to jealousy *those who are* my flesh and save some of them."[176] Indeed, an enthusiasm for learning the Hebrew language is a powerful tool in this respect.

Finally, many people do crosswords and other puzzles to keep their minds sharp; we have an additional mental challenge, namely digging deep into Hebrew!

הַרְחֶב־פִּיךָ וַאֲמַלְאֵהוּ

Psalm 81:10 "Open your mouth wide, and I will fill it"

---

[175] The "kh" at the end of *Tanakh* and "k" of "*Ketuvim*" reflect the alternative readings of the letter *kaf*.
[176] Romans 11:14

English (with transliterations)	Hebrew	
	No vowels	With vowels
wonderful (pel-e)	פלא	פֶּלֶא
Mighty God (El Gib-bor)	אל גבור	אֵל גִּבּוֹר
the beginning and the end (ha-rosh v'ha-sof)	הראש והסוף	הָרֹאשׁ וְהַסּוֹף
You created all things (atah bara-tah hakol)	אתה בראת הכול	אַתָּה בָּרָאתָ הַכֹּל
worthy (ra-oo-ee)	ראוי	רָאוּי
You [are] worthy	ראוי אתה	רָאוּי אַתָּה
worthy [is] the Lamb	ראוי השה	רָאוּי הַשֶּׂה
The Lion (ha-ar-ey-eh)	האריה	הָאַרְיֵה
From the tribe of Judah (mi-shevet y'hoodah)	משבט יהודה	מִשֵּׁבֶט יְהוּדָה
Root of David (sho-resh Da-vid)	שורש דוד	שׁוֹרֶשׁ דָּוִד
Glory of Your people Israel (Tif-eret yis-rael am-mekha)	תפארת ישראל עמך	תִּפְאֶרֶת יִשְׂרָאֵל עַמְּךָ
Lord Jesus the Messiah (Adon Yeshua Ha-Ma-shee-akh)	אדון ישוע המשיח	אָדוֹן יֵשׁוּעַ הַמָּשִׁיחַ

Further Resources

There is much material available online, both on websites and YouTube videos. It is always preferable to listen to pronunciation by native speakers, especially bearing in mind that English transliterations, such as in this book, have their limitations. The Bible Society of Israel presents Hebrew audio New Testament Bible reading videos on YouTube.

While preparing this book, I have come across an excellent website, Abarim-Publications.com. This goes into great detail about the etymology of Hebrew Bible names.

You can easily go to Bible Hub to find an Old Testament verse you are looking for in English, and then go to the Hebrew page where each Hebrew word in the Bible is translated. There are online modern English-Hebrew dictionary websites.

For those of you who want to go forward with a more academic based approach to learning Hebrew, there is the website "Hebrew4Christians." It is the result of years of hard work by John J. Parsons and offers plenty of free resources for personal use.

The Rev John H. Dobson has written, "Learn Biblical Hebrew,"[177] which includes an audio CD-ROM. If you are prepared to invest some hours a week in learning to read the Old Testament and understanding its Hebrew content, then it is worth checking the reviews for that book.

For readers who would like to press forward and learn modern Hebrew, you may like to invest in the book, "Modern

---

[177] Baker Academic, 1999

Hebrew, An Essential Grammar" by Lewis Glinert.[178] If you want a more casual approach to learning some modern Hebrew, there are many online resources and those aimed at beginners can be followed, if you like, by those designed for children.

The biography of Eliezer Ben-Yehuda, who revived the Hebrew language: "Tongue of the Prophets,"[179] by Robert St. John gives a good idea of how the revival of the language was achieved. When I last checked, it appeared to be out of print, but you may see it second-hand somewhere.

If you are interested in the Pharisees, Sadducees, and the Sanhedrin, it is invaluable to look at "The Life and Times of Jesus the Messiah" by Alfred Edersheim.

Please contact me via my website: fresholivepress.com if you have any questions or comments concerning these lessons. The website links to a number of recordings and transcripts of sermons by Robert, and these have a Jewish Messianic flavour. My companion book is also available through the website. It is written to equip intercessors to pray for Israel, as she approaches the "Time of Jacob's Trouble." It is entitled, "Exploring the End Times and Interceding for Israel."

---

[178] Routledge, 1991
[179] Wilshire Book Co, U.S. 1972

Exploring the End Times and Interceding for Israel

Rosamund Weissman

Dark clouds are drawing ever nearer to Israel, as the storm brews up around her, and the Time of Jacob's Trouble approaches.

Those who pray for Israel do not need a book with formulated prayers. That is the role of the Holy Spirit. What is needed is written material to illuminate the mystery ahead, both for Israel and for the whole world. The Lord will do the rest.

Setting the scene for the Time of Jacob's Trouble is best approached with an eye for detail. This background will show us how to engage with the subject of the End Times and will help us to focus on the people of Jacob. It is a struggle to pray into a situation which we find mysterious.

Jesus tells us to watch and pray; for this we require understanding about what we are watching out for. We need to discern the significance of what is happening on the world stage, as well as what is on the horizon for Israel.

Through explanations about the End Times and glimpses into Israeli society, you will find it easier to connect with Israel in prayer in these last days.

Available via fresholivepress.com